Letters
from God
for Men

Presented to:

_____

Presented by:

_____

Date:

_____

Letters *from* God *for* MEN

God's Faithful Promises for You

HARVEST HOUSE PUBLISHERS

EUGENE, OREGON

Letters from God for Men
ISBN 0-7369-1256-8
Copyright © 2004 by GRQ Ink, Inc.

Published by Harvest House Publishers
Eugene, OR 97402
www.harvesthousepublishers.com

Developed by GRQ Ink, Inc.
Manuscript written by Kyle Lennart Olund
Cover and text design by Whisner Design Group
Composition by Educational Publishing Concepts, Inc.

Printed in China. 04 05 06 07 08 09 10 / RDS / 7 6 5 4 3 2 1

A LETTER FROM GOD

Dear Loved One,

Why should you worry about anything as long as you walk with Me? No one loves you more than I do. No one cares about your life more than I do. No one watches over you more than I do. No one wants a relationship with you more than I do.

I am God over all your life—your career, your marriage, and your family. From the time you wake up in the morning to the time you finally rest your head on the pillow at night, I trust that you will feel My presence. I will be with you every step of the way to bring you peace and to give you wisdom, strength, and encouragement.

With greatest love,

Your Father and Your Friend

> God has come to save me.
> I will trust in him and not be afraid.
> The LORD GOD is my strength and my song; he has become my salvation.
>
> ISAIAH 12:2 NLT

Contents

My Gift to You	8
Walk with a Spiritual Swagger	12
Seek Wise Counsel	14
Seeing Things Through	18
I Will Walk by Your Side	20
Point Your Children to Me	24
Everyday Encounters	26
Live and Give from the Heart	30
Taking Care of Business	32
I Will Rescue You	36
I Am Sufficient for You	40
Lead with Confidence	44
How You Fit into My Plan	46
Put Your Trust in Me	50
Handling Money	54
My Witness	56
Cast All Your Cares on Me	58
I Know Your Needs	62
Can You Hear My Voice?	64
Made in My Image	68
The Joy of Giving	70
New Beginnings	74
A Man of God	76
I Made You	80
Take Heart	82
A Passionate Marriage	86
The Power of Prayer	88
I Am Building a Mansion for You	90
My Helper Sent to You	92
Honor Your Marriage Vows	96

Rest for Your Weary Soul 100

True Wealth 104

Lean Fully on Me 106

Made to Serve 110

True Love 112

Strength in Times of Weakness 116

Live Victoriously 118

The Best Is Yet to Come 122

Talk to Me; I Am Listening 124

Feed My Sheep 126

True Success 128

Making Tough Decisions 132

Know That I Am God 134

The Power of Two or More 138

Continue to Bear Fruit 140

Sticking Closer than a Brother 144

A Personal Handbook on Life 146

Set Your Sights High 150

Working from a Clean Slate 152

Always the Best Option 156

What Keeps You Going 158

Deflecting All Praise to Me 162

Following My Marching Orders 164

Doing Right at All Times 168

Keep All Things in Perspective 170

Enjoy My Creation 174

Passing Along Grace 176

Never Give Up 180

A Heart Ready to Burst 182

Seek This at Any Cost 186

Letters *from* **God** *for* **MEN**

My Gift to You

My peace is more than sufficient for you.

Dear Precious One,

Your mind is filled daily with myriad things that overwhelm you. You have deadlines to meet, budgets to plan, meetings to attend. You face mortgage payments, family responsibilities, church commitments, and many other things. You're left wondering whether you will ever be able to breathe easily again. I have one word for you: *come*.

Come to me, you who are burdened and tired, and I will give you rest. Don't let others lead you to believe that peace will only come after you graduate from college. Or when you finally land that perfect job. Or when your kids move out. Or when you retire. Peace doesn't come from external experiences or because of your plans. True peace is found in Me, and I will give it to you abundantly. All you have to do is ask for it, so come.

Abundantly,

The Prince of Peace

> The Lord gives strength to his people;
> the Lord blesses his people with peace.
> Psalm 29:11 NCV

*May the LORD be good
to you and give you peace.*
NUMBERS 6:26 CEV

You, the LORD's people, will live in peace,
calm and secure, even if hailstones
flatten forests and cities.
ISAIAH 32:18-19 CEV

Behold, I give to him My covenant of peace.
NUMBERS 25:12 NKJV

Stop quarreling with God! If you agree with
him, you will have peace at last, and things
will go well for you.
JOB 22:21 NLT

But the good man—what a different story!
For the good man—the blameless, the
upright, the man of peace—he has a
wonderful future ahead of him. For him there
is a happy ending.
PSALM 37:37 TLB

Grace and peace to you from God our Father
and the Lord Jesus Christ.
1 CORINTHIANS 1:3 NCV

Peace

Peace

Grace to you and peace from God our Father and the Lord Jesus Christ.

2 CORINTHIANS 1:2 NASB

O that thou hadst hearkened to my commandments! then had thy peace been as a river, and thy righteousness as the waves of the sea.

ISAIAH 48:18

How beautiful on the mountains are the feet of those who bring good news of peace and salvation, the news that the God of Israel reigns!

ISAIAH 52:7 NLT

There will be no joy and happiness in the orchards and no songs or shouts of joy in the vineyards. No one makes wine in the winepresses, because I have put an end to shouts of joy.

ISAIAH 16:10 NCV

I will both lay me down in peace, and sleep: for thou, LORD, only makest me dwell in safety.

PSALM 4:8

I give you peace, the kind of peace that only I can give. It isn't like the peace that this world can give. So don't be worried or afraid.

JOHN 14:27 CEV

Look, there on the mountains,
the feet of one who brings good news,
who proclaims peace!
Celebrate your festivals, O Judah,
and fulfill your vows.
No more will the wicked invade you;
they will be completely destroyed.

NAHUM 1:15 NIV

The steadfast of mind You will keep in
perfect peace,
Because he trusts in You.

ISAIAH 26:3 NASB

Let the peace of God rule in your hearts, to
which also you were called in one body;
and be thankful.

COLOSSIANS 3:15 NKJV

Finally, brethren, farewell. Be perfect, be of
good comfort, be of one mind, live in peace;
and the God of love and peace
shall be with you.

2 CORINTHIANS 13:11

Grace *be* to you, and peace,
from God our Father, and
from the Lord Jesus Christ.

EPHESIANS 1:2

My Gift to You

11

WALK WITH A SPIRITUAL SWAGGER

You have nothing to fear.

Dear Warrior,

You never should be ashamed to be called one of My own. You are a follower of the one true God, the creator of heaven and earth, the Alpha and the Omega. I am a warrior, and I expect nothing less from My troops.

Put on the full spiritual armor with which I have provided you, stand strong in My name, and go forward confidently and live out your calling. Moses felt unworthy of doing anything, but I made him a great leader. David was just a boy, yet I gave him the courage to conquer Goliath. I helped Gideon overcome a mighty army after I reduced his troops from ten thousand to three hundred. I am that same God, and I will empower you just the same.

With strength,

Almighty God

> Do not throw away this confident trust in the Lord, no matter what happens. Remember the great reward it brings you!
>
> HEBREWS 10:35 NLT

For the LORD shall be thy confidence, and shall keep thy foot from being taken.
PROVERBS 3:26

The wicked are edgy with guilt,
ready to run off
even when no one's after them;
Honest people are relaxed and confident,
bold as lions.
PROVERBS 28:1 THE MESSAGE

By awesome deeds in righteousness
You will answer us,
O God of our salvation,
You who are the confidence of all
the ends of the earth,
And of the far-off seas.
PSALM 65:5 NKJV

It is better to trust the LORD
than to put confidence in people.
It is better to trust the LORD
than to put confidence in princes.
PSALM 118:8-9 NLT

Christ now gives us courage and confidence,
so that we can come to God by faith.
EPHESIANS 3:12 CEV

Boldness

SEEK WISE COUNSEL

Wisdom is your most valuable asset.

Dear Son,

I know that you attended school for several years. I know the numerous books you read, the countless hours you studied, and the many tests you took. When you began your career, you worked hard to get where you are. Don't stop now, though. There is still so much for you to learn and understand, and there is much more wisdom for you to gain.

Seek wisdom at all times. Be as diligent and purposeful in its pursuit as was Solomon. Read My Word, break it down, and ask Me every question that fills your mind. Be in communion with fellow believers, especially those who are older than you, who can pass along their wisdom. I love to see you thirsting for My wisdom, because it shows how much you love Me.

With great love,

Your Father

You desire honesty from the heart,
so you can teach me to be wise in my inmost being.
PSALM 51:6 NLT

Solomon was brilliant.
God had blessed him with
insight and understanding.
1 KINGS 4:29 CEV

How blessed is the man who finds wisdom
And the man who gains understanding.
For her profit is better than the
profit of silver
And her gain better than fine gold.
PROVERBS 3:13-14 NASB

The Lord God has given me his words of
wisdom so that I may know what I should say
to all these weary ones. Morning by morning
he wakens me and opens my understanding
to his will.
ISAIAH 50:4 TLB

Give me now wisdom and knowledge, that I
may go out and come in before this people:
for who can judge this thy people,
that is so great?
2 CHRONICLES 1:10

Teach us how short our lives really are
so that we may be wise.
PSALM 90:12 NCV

Wisdom

Wisdom

*How can men be wise? The only way to begin is
by reverence for God. For growth in wisdom comes
from obeying his laws. Praise his name forever.*
PSALM 111:10 TLB

For I want you to understand what really
matters, so that you may live pure and
blameless lives until Christ returns.
PHILIPPIANS 1:10 NLT

God gives helpful advice
to everyone who obeys him
and protects all of those
who live as they should.
PROVERBS 2:7 CEV

When pride comes, then comes dishonor,
But with the humble is wisdom.
PROVERBS 11:2 NASB

Too much pride causes trouble.
Be sensible and take advice.
PROVERBS 13:10 CEV

Buy the truth, and do not sell *it*,
Also wisdom and instruction and understanding.
PROVERBS 23:23 NKJV

Prefer my life-disciplines over chasing money,
and God-knowledge over a lucrative career.
For Wisdom is better than all the
trappings of wealth;
nothing you could wish for
holds a candle to her.

PROVERBS 8:10-11 THE MESSAGE

I keep asking that the God of our Lord Jesus
Christ, the glorious Father, may give you the
Spirit of wisdom and revelation, so that you
may know him better.

EPHESIANS 1:17 NIV

And the spirit of the LORD shall rest upon him,
the spirit of wisdom and understanding, the
spirit of counsel and might, the spirit of
knowledge and of the fear of the LORD.

ISAIAH 11:2

If you need wisdom—if you want to know
what God wants you to do—ask him,
and he will gladly tell you.
He will not resent your asking.

JAMES 1:5 NLT

Seek Wise
Counsel

SEEING THINGS THROUGH

Don't give up — keep trying!

My Own,

There is no doubt that it is easier to give up on something than it is to stick with it to the end. Consider the act of teaching a child how to catch a ball. When at first you lightly toss the ball to him, does he catch it? Not unless he is fortunate enough to have it land in his arms after it has hit his hand, ricocheted off his forehead, and bounced back up from the ground. No, usually it takes many, many tosses and misses before he catches it intentionally.

That's the kind of commitment I hope you make in everything you do. When you make and honor such a commitment, you will surely be rewarded. How I love to see your dedication to your marriage, your children, and your job, and especially as you work out your faith serving Me.

With abundant encouragement,

Your Biggest Fan

> He that shall endure unto the end,
> the same shall be saved.
> MATTHEW 24:13

Anyone who puts a hand to the plow and then looks back is not fit for the Kingdom of God.
LUKE 9:62 NLT

Pray in the Spirit at all times with all kinds of prayers, asking for everything you need. To do this you must always be ready and never give up. Always pray for all God's people.
EPHESIANS 6:18 NCV

Everyone will hate you because of me. But if you keep on being faithful right to the end, you will be saved.
MARK 13:13 CEV

You must encourage one another each day. And you must keep on while there is still a time that can be called "today." If you don't, then sin may fool some of you and make you stubborn.
HEBREWS 3:13 CEV

I am warning you ahead of time, dear brothers, so that you can watch out and not be carried away by the mistakes of these wicked men, lest you yourselves become mixed up too.
2 PETER 3:17 TLB

Commitment

I Will Walk by Your Side

Spiritual help is all around.

Dear Friend,

I know at times you feel as if you are all alone, but that feeling is further from the truth than you can imagine. As My follower, you have a number of examples of My presence in your life. In addition to always being present with you, I have sent to you the Holy Spirit, who guides, encourages, and comforts you. But there is one more form of My companionship that is often overlooked or taken for granted—the special communion you can have with other believers.

I love to be with you, and I long for you to seek Me with all your heart. In fact, I created you so we could be in relationship with each other.

I love you,

Your God

> God will surely do this for you, for he always does just what he says, and he is the one who invited you into this wonderful friendship with his Son, even Christ our Lord.
>
> 1 Corinthians 1:9 TLB

Now you are Christ's body, and individually members of it.
1 CORINTHIANS 12:27 NASB

Your ears shall hear a word behind you, saying,
"This *is* the way, walk in it,"
Whenever you turn to the right hand
Or whenever you turn to the left.
ISAIAH 30:21 NKJV

They spent their time learning from the
apostles, and they were like family to each
other. They also broke bread and prayed
together.
ACTS 2:42 CEV

They begged us again and again for the
gracious privilege of sharing in the gift for the
Christians in Jerusalem.
2 CORINTHIANS 8:4 NLT

James, Peter, and John, who seemed to be the
leaders, understood that God had given me
this special grace, so they accepted Barnabas
and me. They agreed that they would go to the
Jewish people and that we should go to those
who are not Jewish.
GALATIANS 2:9 NCV

Companionship

Companionship

*Now I have given up everything else — I have
found it to be the only way to really know Christ
and to experience the mighty power that brought
him back to life again, and to find out what it
means to suffer and to die with him.*

PHILIPPIANS 3:10 TLB

We do not lose heart. Though outwardly we are
wasting away, yet inwardly we are being renewed
day by day. For our light and momentary troubles
are achieving for us an eternal glory that far
outweighs them all. So we fix our eyes not on what
is seen, but on what is unseen. For what is seen is
temporary, but what is unseen is eternal.

2 CORINTHIANS 4:16-18 NIV

We do not preach ourselves, but Jesus Christ as
Lord, and ourselves as your servants for Jesus' sake.
For God, who said, "Let light shine out of
darkness," made his light shine in our hearts to give
us the light of the knowledge of the glory of God in
the face of Christ.

2 CORINTHIANS 4:5-6 NIV

I shall walk before the LORD
In the land of the living.

PSALM 116:9 NASB

When I walk into the thick of trouble,
keep me alive in the angry turmoil.
With one hand strike my foes,
With your other hand save me.

PSALM 138:7 THE MESSAGE

Yea, though I walk through the valley of the
shadow of death, I will fear no evil: for thou *art*
with me; thy rod and thy staff
they comfort me.

PSALM 23:4

We are telling you about what we ourselves
have actually seen and heard, so that you may
have fellowship with us. And our fellowship is
with the Father and with his Son, Jesus Christ.

1 JOHN 1:3 NLT

The LORD has told you, human, what is good;
he has told you what he wants from you:
to do what is right to other people,
love being kind to others,
and live humbly,
obeying your God.

MICAH 6:8 NCV

I Will Walk
by Your Side

POINT YOUR CHILDREN TO ME

Raising children is a parent's greatest obligation.

My Child,

I don't have to remind you that you have a great responsibility in raising children. From the day they are born, you watch out for them, you provide for them, and you love them. Still, your most important duties are to teach them about Me, pray for them, and lead them toward a personal faith.

Sometimes they may stray, disappoint you, or even turn their backs on Me. Don't give up on them. Keep loving them and believing that they will return. That is what I have done with you. Every time you have left Me and gone against My teaching, I have waited for you, ready to take you once again in My arms and lavishly pour out My love on you.

With a love that never runs dry,

Abba

> Parents, don't be hard on your children.
> Raise them properly. Teach them
> and instruct them about the Lord.
> EPHESIANS 6:4 CEV

Train up a child in the way he should go: and when he is old, he will not depart from it.

PROVERBS 22:6

But watch out! Be very careful never to forget what you have seen God doing for you. May his miracles have a deep and permanent effect upon your lives! Tell your children and your grandchildren about the glorious miracles he did.

DEUTERONOMY 4:9 TLB

These commandments that I give you today are to be upon your hearts. Impress them on your children. Talk about them when you sit at home and when you walk along the road, when you lie down and when you get up. Tie them as symbols on your hands and bind them on your foreheads. Write them on the doorframes of your houses and on your gates.

DEUTERONOMY 6:6-9 NIV

From a child thou hast known the holy scriptures, which are able to make thee wise unto salvation through faith which is in Christ Jesus.

2 TIMOTHY 3:15

Family

Everyday Encounters

Don't miss out on any God-moments.

Dear Seeker,

Every day is a gift from me. Do you believe that? I know that you do not always wake up with anticipation of what each day will bring. Some days it seems impossible for you even to face the world. If you don't, though, you'll miss out on something great, because I always have something special in store for you.

Today is an adventure, if only you will embrace it. The most action-packed movie you have ever seen or thrilling book you have read pales in significance to what you can experience through Me. Make sure you are with Me every day of your life, because you definitely don't want to miss out on one minute with Me.

Always there to greet you,

Your Bright Morning Star

> This is what the LORD says:
> "Stand at the crossroads and look;
> ask for the ancient paths,
> ask where the good way is, and walk in it,
> and you will find rest for your souls.
> But you said, 'We will not walk in it.'"
> JEREMIAH 6:16 NIV

*As for me, I will walk
in my integrity;
Redeem me and be
merciful to me.*
PSALM 26:11 NKJV

Be very careful how you live. Don't live like
foolish people but like wise people. Make the
most of your opportunities because
these are evil days.
EPHESIANS 5:15-16 GOD'S WORD

Surely goodness and lovingkindness will
follow me all the days of my life,
And I will dwell in the
house of the LORD forever.
PSALM 23:6 NASB

When I am afraid,
I put my trust in you.
PSALM 56:3 NLT

He that walketh with wise *men* shall be wise:
but a companion of fools shall be destroyed.
PROVERBS 13:20

Those who trust in themselves are foolish,
but those who live wisely will be kept safe.
PROVERBS 28:26 NCV

Daily Walk

Daily Walk

When Abram was ninety-nine years old, the LORD appeared to him and said, "I am God Almighty; walk before me and be blameless."
GENESIS 17:1 NIV

I will walk among you, and will be your God, and ye shall be my people. I am the LORD your God, which brought you forth out of the land of Egypt, that ye should not be their bondmen; and I have broken the bands of your yoke, and made you go upright.
LEVITICUS 26:12-13

No lion will lurk along its course,
nor will there be any other dangers;
only the redeemed will travel there.
ISAIAH 35:9 TLB

Listen, everyone!
Whether you ride a donkey
with a padded saddle or have to walk.
Even those who carry water to the animals
will tell you, "The LORD has won victories,
and so has Israel."
JUDGES 5:10-11 CEV

If we live in the light, as God does, we share in life with each other. And the blood of his Son Jesus washes all our sins away.
1 JOHN 1:7 CEV

Oh, wash yourselves! Be clean! Let me no
longer see you doing all these wicked things;
quit your evil ways. Learn to do good, to be
fair, and to help the poor,
the fatherless, and widows.

ISAIAH 1:16-17 TLB

How terrible it will be for those people who
go down to Egypt for help.
They think horses will save them.
They think their many chariots
and strong horsemen will save them.
But they don't trust God,
the Holy One of Israel,
or ask the LORD for help.

ISAIAH 31:1 NCV

Get to know the God of your ancestors.
Worship and serve him with your whole
heart and with a willing mind. For the LORD
sees every heart and understands and knows
every plan and thought. If you seek him, you
will find him. But if you forsake him,
he will reject you forever.

1 CHRONICLES 28:9 NLT

Everyday
Encounters

LIVE AND GIVE FROM THE HEART

Always reach out to others.

Dear Loved One,

I know you are aware that there are hurting people in this world, but did you know that some of those individuals are ones with whom you work and live? Without you even knowing it, there are people in your life who need someone to show them love and to encourage them to keep going on.

Whatever their necessity, consider that you may be just what they need—you may be My answer to their prayers. You may have the money to help someone through a financial crisis. You may be the friend who someone needs to confide in. Or you may simply have the smile to turn a coworker's day around. Keep your eyes open today, and you will notice many opportunities to give.

With an unlimited surplus of love,

Your Generous Father

Give, and it will be given to you. A good measure, pressed down, shaken together and running over, will be poured into your lap. For with the measure you use, it will be measured to you.

LUKE 6:38 NIV

Give to him who asks of you,
and do not turn away from him
who wants to borrow from you.
MATTHEW 5:42 NASB

Heal the sick, raise the dead,
cure the lepers, and cast out demons.
Give as freely as you have received!
MATTHEW 10:8 TLB

Jesus answered, "If you want to be perfect,
go, sell your possessions and give to the
poor, and you will have treasure in heaven.
Then come, follow me."
MATTHEW 19:21 NIV

Servants who don't know what their master
wants them to do will not be beaten so hard
for doing wrong. If God has been generous
with you, he will expect you to serve him
well. But if he has been more than generous,
he will expect you to serve him even better.
LUKE 12:48 CEV

Take heed that you do not do your charitable
deeds before men, to be seen by them.
Otherwise you have no reward from your
Father in heaven.
MATTHEW 6:1 NKJV

Compassion

Taking Care of Business

Your hard work will be blessed.

Dear Son,

I know that some days are harder for you than others during the workweek. Always strive for your best and be encouraged in your efforts on the good days and on the not-so-good days. Remember who you work for—not man, but Me. Your labor is never in vain.

I have given you many gifts and abilities, and you honor Me in how you use them. So the next time you are asked to give a presentation, put together one that is more comprehensive and engaging than what has ever been done before. Whatever you do at work, do it to My glory, and you will always be satisfied in your job.

With all the strength you need,

Almighty God

Six days you shall labor and do all your work.
DEUTERONOMY 5:13 NASB

Whatever work you do, do your best, because you are going to the grave, where there is no working, no planning, no knowledge, and no wisdom.
ECCLESIASTES 9:10 NCV

May our Lord Jesus Christ himself and God our Father, who has loved us and given us everlasting comfort and hope which we don't deserve, comfort your hearts with all comfort, and help you in every good thing you say and do.
2 THESSALONIANS 2:16-17 TLB

The elders who direct the affairs of the church well are worthy of double honor, especially those whose work is preaching and teaching. For the Scripture says, "Do not muzzle the ox while it is treading out the grain," and "The worker deserves his wages."
1 TIMOTHY 5:17-18 NIV

Thou believest that there is one God; thou doest well: the devils also believe, and tremble. But wilt thou know, O vain man, that faith without works is dead?
JAMES 2:19-20

Work

Work

*It is for this we labor and strive, because we have
fixed our hope on the living God, who is the
Savior of all men, especially of believers.*
1 TIMOTHY 4:10 NASB

Don't work for the food that spoils. Work for the
food that stays good always and gives eternal life.
The Son of Man will give you this food, because on
him God the Father has put his power.
JOHN 6:27 NCV

Surely he says this for us, doesn't he? Yes, this was
written for us, because when the plowman plows
and the thresher threshes, they ought to do so in
the hope of sharing in the harvest.
1 CORINTHIANS 9:10 NIV

My dear friends, you always obeyed when I was
with you. Now that I am away, you should obey
even more. So work with fear and trembling to
discover what it really means to be saved. God is
working in you to make you willing and able to obey
him. Do everything without grumbling or arguing.
PHILIPPIANS 2:12-14 CEV

Having your conduct honorable among the Gentiles,
that when they speak against you as evildoers, they
may, by *your* good works which they observe,
glorify God in the day of visitation.
1 PETER 2:12 NKJV

Take a lesson from the ants, you lazy fellow.
Learn from their ways and be wise! For
though they have no king to make them
work, yet they labor hard all summer,
gathering food for the winter.

PROVERBS 6:6-8 TLB

Even now the reaper draws his wages,
even now he harvests the crop for eternal
life, so that the sower and the reaper
may be glad together.

JOHN 4:36 NIV

You surely know that you should follow our
example. We didn't waste our time loafing,
and we didn't accept food from anyone
without paying for it. We didn't want to be a
burden to any of you, so night and day we
worked as hard as we could.

2 THESSALONIANS 3:7-8 CEV

God has made us what we are. In Christ
Jesus, God made us to do good works,
which God planned in advance
for us to live our lives doing.

EPHESIANS 2:10 NCV

Taking Care
of Business

I WILL RESCUE YOU

You will be victorious.

My Own,

Think of yourself in the midst of a great battle, surrounded by an enemy who is closing in on you with an overwhelming arsenal. It looks as though you are greatly outnumbered and that your foe will soon overtake you! But what he does not know is that you have an Ally ready to rescue you.

I am your Ally, your Deliverer. You have nothing to fear, for I will help you defeat your adversaries and will rescue you in mighty fashion, just as I have done for countless believers before you. I am your Shield and your Refuge. Take shelter in Me and know that I will save you.

Ready to deliver you,

Your Redeemer

The angel of the Lord by night opened the prison doors, and brought them forth.
ACTS 5:19

You are my hiding place.
You protect me from my
troubles and fill me with
songs of salvation.
PSALM 32:7 NCV

He is my loving ally and my fortress,
my tower of safety, my deliverer.
He stands before me as a shield,
and I take refuge in him.
He subdues the nations under me.
PSALM 144:2 NLT

The Lord stayed with me and gave me
strength so I could fully tell the Good News
to all those who are not Jews. So I was saved
from the lion's mouth. The Lord will save me
when anyone tries to hurt me, and he will
bring me safely to his heavenly kingdom.
Glory forever and ever be the Lord's. Amen.
2 TIMOTHY 4:17-18 NCV

The LORD is my rock, my protection,
my Savior. My God is my rock.
I can run to him for safety.
He is my shield and my saving strength,
my defender.
PSALM 18:2 NCV

Deliverance

Deliverance

*God has sent me here to keep you
and your families alive so that you will
become a great nation.*
GENESIS 45:7 NLT

It shall come to pass, *that* whosoever shall call on
the name of the LORD shall be delivered: for in
mount Zion and in Jerusalem shall be deliverance,
as the LORD hath said, and in the remnant
whom the LORD shall call.
JOEL 2:32

My God sent His angel and shut the lions' mouths
and they have not harmed me, inasmuch as I was
found innocent before Him; and also toward you, O
king, I have committed no crime.
DANIEL 6:22 NASB

The Lord GOD has put his Spirit in me,
because the LORD has appointed me to
tell the good news to the poor.
He has sent me to comfort those whose
hearts are broken,
to tell the captives they are free,
and to tell the prisoners they are released.
ISAIAH 61:1 NCV

Suddenly there was a great earthquake, so that the foundations of the prison were shaken; and immediately all the doors were opened and everyone's chains were loosed.

ACTS 16:26 NKJV

The Spirit of the Lord *is* upon me, because he hath anointed me to preach the gospel to the poor; he hath sent me to heal the brokenhearted, to preach deliverance to the captives, and recovering of sight to the blind, to set at liberty them that are bruised.

LUKE 4:18

Suddenly an angel from the Lord appeared, and light flashed around in the cell. The angel poked Peter in the side and woke him up.
Then he said, "Quick! Get up!"
The chains fell off his hands, and the angel said, "Get dressed and put on your sandals." Peter did what he was told. Then the angel said, "Now put on your coat and follow me."

ACTS 12:7-8 CEV

I Will
Rescue You

I Am Sufficient for You

My blessings will overflow for you.

Dear Loved One,

In this world there are many things that seem to yell out to you: "Buy me," "You need me," or "You can't get by without me." Soon you start believing that, without more, your life is not complete and you are not whole. My son, you don't need more of the things of this world; you need more of Me.

I am everything you will ever need. I am strength for the weary. I am food for the hungry. I am drink for the thirsty. I am comfort for the hurting. Things in this world will let you down because they are not enough. But I am more than enough.

All you will ever need,

Your Provider

He said unto me, My grace is sufficient for thee: for my strength is made perfect in weakness. Most gladly therefore will I rather glory in my infirmities, that the power of Christ may rest upon me.

2 CORINTHIANS 12:9

Our lives are a fragrance presented by Christ to God. But this fragrance is perceived differently by those being saved and by those perishing.

2 CORINTHIANS 2:15 NLT

Look closely at yourselves. Test yourselves
to see if you are living in the faith.
You know that Jesus Christ is in you
—unless you fail the test.

2 CORINTHIANS 13:5 NCV

"I decree that everyone throughout my
kingdom should tremble with fear
before the God of Daniel.
For he is the living God,
and he will endure forever.
His kingdom will never be destroyed,
and his rule will never end.
He rescues and saves his people;
he performs miraculous signs and wonders
in the heavens and on earth.
He has rescued Daniel
from the power of the lions."

DANIEL 6:26-27 NLT

"Don't be upset. Just trust me
and everything will be all right."

LUKE 8:50 THE MESSAGE

Fulfillment

Fulfillment

*If we are thrown into the blazing furnace, the God
we serve is able to save us from it, and he will
rescue us from your hand, O king. But even if he
does not, we want you to know, O king, that we
will not serve your gods or worship
the image of gold you have set up.*

DANIEL 3:17-18 NIV

Through their faith they defeated kingdoms. They
did what was right, received God's promises, and
shut the mouths of lions. They stopped great fires
and were saved from being killed with swords. They
were weak, and yet were made strong. They were
powerful in battle and defeated other armies.

HEBREWS 11:33-34 NCV

I am suffering now because I tell the Good News,
but I am not ashamed, because I know Jesus, the
One in whom I have believed. And I am sure he is
able to protect what he has trusted me
with until that day.

2 TIMOTHY 1:12 NCV

The Spirit helps us with our weakness. We do not
know how to pray as we should. But the Spirit
himself speaks to God for us, even begs God for us
with deep feelings that words cannot explain.

ROMANS 8:26 NCV

All of God lives in Christ fully (even when
Christ was on earth), and you have a full
and true life in Christ, who is ruler
over all rulers and powers.

COLOSSIANS 2:9-10 NCV

The time is coming when one of David's
descendants will be the signal for
the people of all nations to come together.
They will follow his advice, and his
own nation will become famous.

ISAIAH 11:10 CEV

These things I have written to you who believe
in the name of the Son of God, so that you may
know that you have eternal life.

1 JOHN 5:13 NASB

Not that we are competent of ourselves to
claim anything as coming from us; our
competence is from God, who has made us
competent to be ministers of a new covenant,
not of letter but of spirit; for the letter kills,
but the Spirit gives life.

2 CORINTHIANS 3:5-6 NRSV

I Am Sufficient
for You

LEAD WITH CONFIDENCE

Look to Jesus as your mentor.

Dear Follower,

I know that you desire to be a great leader. You seek to motivate people at work to do their best. You try to lead your children by example and to train them up in the way they should go. You want to be a positive influence on people and programs at your church. Do you know how you can be the kind of leader you yearn to be? By following My Son.

Jesus is the great Leader. Study My Word and follow His example. No one is a better motivator; no one understands human nature as fully as He does; no one gave up so much just for another. And no one loves you like He loves you. He loves you and wants you to be the leader you can only be by following Him.

Forever yours,

Your Faithful Leader

> Don't be afraid, for I am with you. Do not be dismayed, for I am your God. I will strengthen you. I will help you. I will uphold you with my victorious right hand.
>
> ISAIAH 41:10 NLT

*I will instruct you and teach
you in the way you should go;
I will counsel you and
watch over you.*
PSALM 32:8 NIV

Anyone who rebels against your command
and does not obey your words in all that you
command him, shall be put to death; only be
strong and courageous.

JOSHUA 1:18 NASB

"So come, I will send you to Pharaoh to
bring my people, the Israelites, out of Egypt."
But Moses said to God, "Who am I that
I should go to Pharaoh, and bring the
Israelites out of Egypt?" He said, "I will be
with you; and this shall be the sign for you
that it is I who sent you: when you have
brought the people out of Egypt, you shall
worship God on this mountain."

EXODUS 3:10-12 NRSV

The LORD shall guide thee continually, and
satisfy thy soul in drought, and make fat thy
bones: and thou shalt be like a watered
garden, and like a spring of water,
whose waters fail not.

ISAIAH 58:11

Leadership

HOW YOU FIT INTO MY PLAN

You are just the person I want.

Dear Child of Mine,

Did you know that you fit perfectly into My plan? I know that you often wonder if you are doing enough for Me, or if you are actually doing what I have called you to do. I want you to know that you—who you are and what you do for a living—are just who I want to carry out My work on earth.

You don't have to go off to the middle of some jungle to be My witness. You don't have to go down to the street corner and start reading the Bible through a megaphone. Just keep doing what you're doing and let others see Me in how you live your life. You are a puzzle piece—unique and vital to My big picture.

In My hands,

Your Maker

> Trust in the LORD with all your heart
> And do not lean on your own understanding.
> In all your ways acknowledge Him,
> And He will make your paths straight.
> PROVERBS 3:5-6 NASB

Teach me to do what you want,
because you are my God.
Let your good Spirit
lead me on level ground.
PSALM 143:10 NCV

Who makes people able to speak or makes
them deaf or unable to speak? Who gives
them sight or makes them blind? Don't you
know that I am the one who does these
things? Now go! When you speak, I will be
with you and give you the words to say.
EXODUS 4:11-12 CEV

This punishment is given at the
command of the holy angels.
It will show to all who live
that God Most High controls all kingdoms
and chooses for their rulers
persons of humble birth.
DANIEL 4:17 CEV

All the inhabitants of the earth *are* reputed as
nothing: and he doeth according to his will in
the army of heaven, and *among* the
inhabitants of the earth: and none can stay his
hand, or say unto him, What doest thou?
DANIEL 4:35

The Will of God

The Will of God

To all who received him, to those who believed
in his name, he gave the right to become children
of God—children born not of natural descent,
nor of human decision or a husband's will,
but born of God.
JOHN 1:12-13 NIV

"I will have mercy on whomever I will have mercy,
and I will have compassion on whomever I will have
compassion." So then *it is* not of him who wills, nor
of him who runs, but of God who shows mercy.
ROMANS 9:15-16 NKJV

The scripture says to Pharaoh, "I have raised you up
for the very purpose of showing my power in you,
so that my name may be proclaimed in all the
earth." So then he has mercy on whomever he
chooses, and he hardens the heart
of whomever he chooses.
ROMANS 9:17-18 NRSV

May your Kingdom come soon.
May your will be done here on earth,
just as it is in heaven.
MATTHEW 6:10 NLT

Do not be foolish, but understand what
the will of the Lord is.
EPHESIANS 5:17 NRSV

God added his testimony by signs and
wonders and various miracles, and by
gifts of the Holy Spirit, distributed
according to his will.

HEBREWS 2:4 NRSV

Let your light shine before men in such a
way that they may see your good works, and
glorify your Father who is in heaven.

MATTHEW 5:16 NASB

If any of you really determines to do God's
will, then you will certainly know whether
my teaching is from God or is merely my
own. Anyone presenting his own ideas is
looking for praise for himself, but anyone
seeking to honor the one who sent him is a
good and true person.

JOHN 7:17-18 TLB

We thank God for you and always mention
you in our prayers. Each time we pray, we
tell God our Father about your faith and
loving work and about your firm
hope in our Lord Jesus Christ.

1 THESSALONIANS 1:2-3 CEV

How You Fit
into My Plan

PUT YOUR TRUST IN ME

I will always catch you.

Dear Son,

Consider a child jumping from a high place into the arms of his father. He has no fear because he knows that his daddy will catch him. More importantly—and even more specifically in his mind—he knows that he will not let him fall. Maybe he was apprehensive for the first couple of leaps, but his faith in his father has grown strong over time.

That is how I hope you see Me—as your loving Father, with My arms open wide, ready to catch you when you jump. I love you and want you to have the greatest, unwavering faith in Me. I will always catch you—so go ahead and jump.

With open arms,

Your Loving Father

I will call upon the Lord,
who is worthy to be praised:
so shall I be saved from mine enemies.

PSALM 18:3

I trusted in your steadfast love;
my heart shall rejoice in
your salvation.

PSALM 13:5 NRSV

Moses answered, "Don't be afraid! Stand still
and you will see the LORD save you today.
You will never see these Egyptians again after
today. You only need to remain calm; the
LORD will fight for you."

EXODUS 14:13-14 NCV

Offer the sacrifices of righteousness,
And put your trust in the LORD.

PSALM 4:5 NKJV

This is the confidence that we have in him,
that, if we ask any thing according to his will,
he heareth us.

1 JOHN 5:14

Those who know your name trust in you, for
you, O LORD, have never abandoned anyone
who searches for you.

PSALM 9:10 NLT

Do not let your hearts be troubled. Believe in
God, believe also in me.

JOHN 14:1 NRSV

Trust

Trust

Some people trust the power of chariots or horses,
but we trust you, LORD God.
Others will stumble and fall,
but we will be strong and stand firm.
PSALM 20:7-8 CEV

Trust in the LORD and do good;
dwell in the land and enjoy safe pasture.
PSALM 37:3 NIV

I am teaching you today—yes,
you—so you will trust in the LORD.
PROVERBS 22:19 NLT

Again, I will put my trust in him. And again, Behold I
and the children which God hath given me.
HEBREWS 2:13

May the God of hope fill you with all joy and peace
as you trust in him, so that you may overflow with
hope by the power of the Holy Spirit.
ROMANS 15:13 NIV

Thou has delivered my soul from death: *wilt* not
thou deliver my feet from falling, that I may walk
before God in the light of the living?
PSALM 56:13

For our heart rejoices in Him,
Because we trust in His holy name.
PSALM 33:21 NASB

I waited patiently for the LORD;
he turned to me and heard my cry.
He lifted me out of the slimy pit,
out of the mud and mire;
he set my feet on a rock
and gave me a firm place to stand.
He put a new song in my mouth,
a hymn of praise to our God.
Many will see and fear
and put their trust in the LORD.
PSALM 40:1-3 NIV

I praise your promises!
I trust you and am not afraid.
No one can harm me.
PSALM 56:4 CEV

Let's see if your idols can do anything for you
when you cry to them for help. They are so
helpless that a breath of wind can knock them
down! But whoever trusts in me will
possess the land and inherit my
holy mountain.
ISAIAH 57:13 NLT

Put Your
Trust in Me

HANDLING MONEY

You have a great responsibility.

My Own,

I wish My people didn't agonize over money so much. I see it over and over—they seek more money, but when they attain it, it is still not enough or it makes them miserable. The problem is that they look at money from the wrong perspective. Please don't make the same mistake. Remember that your money is not yours to begin with. It is Mine, and I have entrusted you with it.

Whether you make a lot of money or just a little, I expect you to use it to My glory. I love to give lavishly to you, but I love even more to see you, in turn, give generously to others in My name.

Abundantly for you,

Your Gracious Father

> Be shepherds of God's flock that is under your care, serving as overseers—not because you must, but because you are willing, as God wants you to be; not greedy for money, but eager to serve.
> I PETER 5:2 NIV

Wealth gotten by vanity shall be diminished: but he that gathereth by labour shall increase.

PROVERBS 13:11

Well done, good and faithful servant! You have been faithful with a few things; I will put you in charge of many things. Come and share your master's happiness!

MATTHEW 25:21 NIV

No one can serve two masters. For you will hate one and love the other, or be devoted to one and despise the other. You cannot serve both God and money.

MATTHEW 6:24 NLT

The love of money causes all kinds of trouble. Some people want money so much that they have given up their faith and caused themselves a lot of pain.

I TIMOTHY 6:10 CEV

On the first day of every week, each one of you should put aside money as you have been blessed. Save it up so you will not have to collect money after I come.

I CORINTHIANS 16:2 NCV

Finances

My Witness

Be proud of your faith.

Dear Beloved,

I never said that following Me would be easy. I know that it is difficult being My ambassador when you are treated like an outsider—especially when it happens in your homeland. But don't give up. Remember that you are never on your own. I have given you many resources to help you be My witness—My Word, the Holy Spirit, fellow believers, the hope of eternal life.

Go forth boldly in My name. Continue speaking out and living your life for the furtherance of My kingdom. And remember, wherever you are—whether on your coffee break at work or on a trip abroad—you will find people who need Me. Thank you for being My witness to them.

With one purpose,

The God of Salvation

> You shall receive power when the Holy Spirit has come upon you; and you shall be witnesses to Me in Jerusalem, and in all Judea and Samaria, and to the end of the earth.
>
> ACTS 1:8 NKJV

I am proud of the good news! It is God's powerful way of saving all people who have faith, whether they are Jews or Gentiles.

ROMANS 1:16 CEV

Do your best to present yourself to God as one approved, a workman who does not need to be ashamed and who correctly handles the word of truth.

2 TIMOTHY 2:15 NIV

The things which you have heard from me in the presence of many witnesses, entrust these to faithful men who will be able to teach others also.

2 TIMOTHY 2:2 NASB

Go and make disciples of all the nations, baptizing them in the name of the Father and the Son and the Holy Spirit. Teach these new disciples to obey all the commands I have given you. And be sure of this: I am with you always, even to the end of the age.

MATTHEW 28:19-20 NLT

If *any man suffer* as a Christian, let him not be ashamed; but let him glorify God on this behalf.

1 PETER 4:16

Witnessing

CAST ALL YOUR CARES ON ME

I can bear all your burdens.

Dear One,

Why do you worry, precious one? Have I ever let you down, or not been able to carry your burdens upon My immeasurably broad shoulders? No, never. Oh, how I long for you to come to Me with all of your concerns. It is not a mark of weakness when you rely on Me—rather, it is a sign of great faith and an example to others of My commitment and power.

How I long for you to run to My arms and pour out your heart to Me. I love you so much, and I desire to prove it to you over and over. So don't worry about anything— be it big or small—but instead trust in My goodness.

In My hands,

Your Heavenly Father

Do not worry about tomorrow; for tomorrow will care for itself. Each day has enough trouble of its own.
MATTHEW 6:34 NASB

Give all your worries and cares to God, for he cares about what happens to you.
1 PETER 5:7 NLT

I am confident of this very thing, that He who began a good work in you will perfect it until the day of Christ Jesus. For it is only right for me to feel this way about you all, because I have you in my heart, since both in my imprisonment and in the defense and confirmation of the gospel, you all are partakers of grace with me.
PHILIPPIANS 1:6-7 NASB

These are the ones sown among thorns; *they are* the ones who hear the word, and the cares of this world, the deceitfulness of riches, and the desires for other things entering in choke the word, and it becomes unfruitful.
MARK 4:18-19 NKJV

"Be on guard so that your hearts are not weighed down with dissipation and drunkenness and the worries of this life, and that day catch you unexpectedly."
LUKE 21:34 NRSV

Worry

Worry

*But when they arrest you, do not worry about
what to say or how to say it. At that time you will
be given what to say, for it will not be you
speaking, but the Spirit of your Father
speaking through you.*
MATTHEW 10:19-20 NIV

So my counsel is: Don't worry about *things*—food,
drink, and clothes. For you already have life and a
body—and they are far more important than what
to eat and wear. Look at the birds! They don't
worry about what to eat—they don't need to sow
or reap or store up food—for your heavenly Father
feeds them. And you are far more valuable to him
than they are. Will all your worries add a
single moment to your life?
MATTHEW 6:25-27 TLB

You do not need to fear
terrors of the night,
arrows that fly during the day,
plagues that roam the dark,
epidemics that strike at noon.
They will not come near you,
even though a thousand may fall dead beside you
or ten thousand at your right side.
PSALM 91:5-7 GOD'S WORD

Remember that I commanded you to be
strong and brave. Don't be afraid, because
the LORD your God will be with you
everywhere you go.

JOSHUA 1:9 NCV

Blessed be the Lord—
day after day he carries us along.
He's our Savior, our God, oh yes!
He's God-for-us, he's God-who-saves-us.

PSALM 68:19-20 THE MESSAGE

Zion, your punishment is over.
The LORD has forced your enemies
to turn and retreat.
Your LORD is King of Israel
and stands at your side;
you don't have to worry
about any more troubles.

ZEPHANIAH 3:15 CEV

Be anxious for nothing, but in everything by
prayer and supplication with thanksgiving let
your requests be made known to God.

PHILIPPIANS 4:6 NASB

Cast All Your
Cares on Me

I KNOW YOUR NEEDS

You are always on My mind.

Dear One,

Does the typical boy usually worry about what he is going to wear in the morning? Does he worry about what he is going to eat? Does he even wonder whether he will have a good day? No, the child jumps out of bed, throws on whatever is available (he may have even worn it the previous day), eats whatever is in the cabinet, and starts to do things that will ensure that he has a great day.

When was the last time you awoke with such reckless enthusiasm for life? I know what your needs are, and I provide for you above what you can imagine. So tonight when you go to bed, have the faith of a little child who cannot wait until the morning comes.

More than you can imagine,

The Lover of Your Soul

> All these things do the nations of the world seek after: and your Father knoweth that ye have need of these things.
> LUKE 12:30

Your Father knows the things you have need of before you ask Him.
MATTHEW 6:8 NKJV

I, the LORD, am your God,
Who brought you up from the land of Egypt;
Open your mouth wide and I will fill it.
PSALM 81:10 NASB

Yes, God will give you much so that you can give away much, and when we take your gifts to those who need them they will break out into thanksgiving and praise to God for your help.
2 CORINTHIANS 9:11 TLB

There was not a needy person among them, for as many as owned lands or houses sold them and brought the proceeds of what was sold. They laid it at the apostles' feet, and it was distributed to each as any had need.
ACTS 4:34-35 NRSV

I pray that God will take care of all your needs with the wonderful blessings that come from Christ Jesus!
PHILIPPIANS 4:19 CEV

Provision of God

CAN YOU HEAR MY VOICE?

I am calling your name.

My Own,

Life can be so overwhelming. As work gets more and more demanding, you wonder how you will ever keep up—or catch up. Family time is often reduced to a quick meal—if even that—or simply a good-night (or good-morning) hug and kiss. Even Sundays grow busier and busier with worship services, church activities, and family dinners. It's easy to get so engrossed in life that you don't notice My voice.

If you listen carefully you can hear Me—amid the din of daily living—calling to you. All you have to do is stop and turn toward Me. Then you will hear what I'm saying to you: *Slow down . . . Come to me . . . I love you.*

Always there for you,

Your Heavenly Father

Hear, O my people, and I will speak; O Israel,
and I will testify against thee:
I *am* God, *even* thy God.
PSALM 50:7

If you will faithfully obey me, you will be my very own people. The whole world is mine, but you will be my holy nation and serve me as priests.
EXODUS 19:5-6 CEV

The LORD used to speak to Moses face to face, as one speaks to a friend. Then he would return to the camp; but his young assistant, Joshua son of Nun, would not leave the tent.
EXODUS 33:11 NRSV

Eli said to Samuel, "Go, lie down; and if he calls you, you shall say, 'Speak, LORD, for your servant is listening.'" So Samuel went and lay down in his place. Now the LORD came and stood there, calling as before, "Samuel! Samuel!" And Samuel said, "Speak, for your servant is listening."
1 SAMUEL 3:9-10 NRSV

Does the LORD really want sacrifices and offerings? No! He doesn't want your sacrifices. He wants you to obey him.
1 SAMUEL 15:22 CEV

Listening to God

Listening to God

*Amend your ways and your doings, and obey the
voice of the LORD your God, and the LORD will
change his mind about the disaster that he has
pronounced against you.*
JEREMIAH 26:13 NRSV

Obey the LORD by doing what I tell you. Then things
will go well for you. And your life will be saved.
JEREMIAH 38:20 NCV

If you follow my statutes and keep my
commandments and observe them faithfully, I will
give you your rains in their season, and the land
shall yield its produce, and the trees of the field
shall yield their fruit.
LEVITICUS 26:3-4 NRSV

What other nation, great or small, has God among
them, as the Lord our God is here among us
whenever we call upon him?
DEUTERONOMY 4:7 TLB

These are the commands and laws you must
carefully obey in the land the LORD, the God of your
ancestors, is giving you. Obey them as long as you
live in the land.
DEUTERONOMY 12:1 NCV

Now listen to me! Even with prophets,
I the LORD communicate by
visions and dreams.
NUMBERS 12:6 NLT

I can't wait to hear what he'll say.
GOD's about to pronounce his people well,
The holy people he loves so much,
so they'll never again live like fools.
PSALM 85:8 THE MESSAGE

The heavens declare the glory of God,
and the sky displays what
his hands have made.
PSALM 19:1 GOD'S WORD

The precepts of the LORD are right,
giving joy to the heart.
The commands of the LORD are radiant,
giving light to the eyes.
PSALM 19:8 NIV

Obey me, and I will be your God, and you
will be my people. Only do as I say,
and all will be well!
JEREMIAH 7:23 NLT

Can You
Hear My Voice?

MADE IN MY IMAGE

You are a spitting image of your Father.

Dear Son,

A number of people experience an identity crisis at some time in their life. You are different though. Your identity problem is not that you don't know who you are, but rather that other people don't recognize who you truly are. You are not Mr. Co-worker, Mr. Athlete, Mr. Church Member, or Mr. Anyone Else. Those identities are the ones whom people observe on the outside. But you live from the inside out.

Your identity is not in what you do, but rather in who you are in Me. When others see you, may they say, "I recognize him. Why, it's clear whose family he belongs to. He's a child of God."

Your one and only,

Abba

You must display a new nature because you are a new person, created in God's likeness—righteous, holy, and true.
EPHESIANS 4:24 NLT

No one can really know what anyone else is thinking, or what he is really like, except that person himself. And no one can know God's thoughts except God's own Spirit.

1 CORINTHIANS 2:11 TLB

God said, Let us make man in our image, after our likeness: and let them have dominion over the fish of the sea, and over the fowl of the air, and over the cattle, and over all the earth, and over every creeping thing that creepeth upon the earth.

GENESIS 1:26

May God himself, the God of peace, sanctify you through and through. May your whole spirit, soul and body be kept blameless at the coming of our Lord Jesus Christ.

1 THESSALONIANS 5:23 NIV

The Lord is the Spirit, and where the Spirit of the Lord is, there is freedom. And we, who with unveiled faces all reflect the Lord's glory, are being transformed into his likeness with ever-increasing glory, which comes from the Lord, who is the Spirit.

2 CORINTHIANS 3:17-18 NIV

Identity

THE JOY OF GIVING

I promise boundless blessings to the giver.

Dear Blessed One,

Everything you have I have graciously given to you. You have been richly blessed. Look around and consider your wealth, which flows far beyond money and possessions — the love of your family and friends, the health of your mind and body, the beauty of your surroundings.

I love your tender heart and your benevolent spirit. When you give generously, you honor Me. When you give of yourself through service and return your tithe to Me, I will pour out My blessings on you.

With abundant love and blessings,

Your Great Provider

"Bring the whole tithe into the storehouse, so that there may be food in My house, and test Me now in this," says the Lord of hosts, "if I will not open for you the windows of heaven and pour out for you a blessing until it overflows."
MALACHI 3:10 NASB

Whoever is kind to the poor
*lends to the L*ORD*,*
and will be repaid in full.
PROVERBS 19:17 NRSV

When people ask you for something, give it
to them. When they want to borrow money,
lend it to them.
MATTHEW 5:42 CEV

When thou doest alms, let not thy left hand
know what thy right hand doeth: That thine
alms may be in secret: and thy Father
which seeth in secret himself shall
reward thee openly.
MATTHEW 6:3-4

You are rich in everything—in faith, in
speaking, in knowledge, in truly wanting to
help, and in the love you learned from us. In
the same way, be strong also in the
grace of giving.
2 CORINTHIANS 8:7 NCV

He is always generous and lends freely.
His descendants are a blessing.
PSALM 37:26 GOD'S WORD

Blessings

Blessings

He who has a generous eye will be blessed,
For he gives of his bread to the poor.
PROVERBS 22:9 NKJV

The people rejoiced at the willing response of their
leaders, for they had given freely and
wholeheartedly to the LORD.
David the king also rejoiced greatly.
1 CHRONICLES 29:9 NIV

The one who blesses others is abundantly blessed;
those who help others are helped.
PROVERBS 11:25 THE MESSAGE

He that giveth unto the poor shall not lack: but he
that hideth his eyes shall have many a curse.
PROVERBS 28:27

Let each one *give* as he purposes in his heart,
not grudgingly or of necessity;
for God loves a cheerful giver.
2 CORINTHIANS 9:7 NKJV

If we have all we need and see one of our own
people in need, we must have pity on that person,
or else we cannot say we love God.
1 JOHN 3:17 CEV

The LORD your God will bless you as he has
promised. You will lend money to many
nations but will never need to borrow! You
will rule many nations, but they will
not rule over you!

DEUTERONOMY 15:6 NLT

My Father has blessed you! Inherit the
kingdom prepared for you from the creation
of the world. I was hungry, and you gave me
something to eat. I was thirsty, and you gave
me something to drink. I was a stranger, and
you took me into your home. I needed
clothes, and you gave me something to
wear. I was sick, and you took care of me. I
was in prison, and you visited me.

MATTHEW 25:34-36 GOD'S WORD

In all this I have given you an example that
by such work we must support the weak,
remembering the words of the Lord Jesus,
for he himself said, "It is more blessed to
give than to receive."

ACTS 20:35 NRSV

The Joy of
Giving

NEW BEGINNINGS

Tomorrow is full of grace.

Dear Beloved,

All seasons are beautiful: The fresh spring, the warm summer, the colorful fall, and the crisp winter. But spring is the most precious of all, for it is My reminder to you that I am a God of new beginnings. No matter how cold the winter or how deep the snow, I will thaw out the earth and bring forth budding trees and flowers, green grass, and new life.

Just as with nature, I bring new beginnings to your life as well. When you're going through wintry experiences in your life, remember that spring will come. Though the chill may seem to last forever, I *will* bring out the warm spring sun and renew your spirit.

With blessings new every morning,

The Lord Your God

Men can only reproduce human life, but the Holy Spirit gives new life from heaven.
JOHN 3:6 TLB

Therefore if any man be in Christ, he is a new creature: old things are passed away; behold, all things are become new.
2 CORINTHIANS 5:17

The winter is past, and the rain is over and gone. The flowers are springing up, and the time of singing birds has come, even the cooing of turtledoves.
SONG OF SONGS 2:11-12 NLT

"Come now, and let us reason together,"
Says the LORD,
"Though your sins are as scarlet,
They shall be as white as snow;
Though they are red like crimson,
They shall be like wool."
ISAIAH 1:18 NASB

I will give them one heart, and put a new spirit within them. And I will take the heart of stone out of their flesh and give them a heart of flesh.
EZEKIEL 11:19 NASB

"Take a walk in every direction and explore the new possessions I am giving you."
GENESIS 13:17 NLT

New Life

A MAN OF GOD

People see Me in you.

Dear Seeker of My Heart,

How important is your reputation? Pretty important, wouldn't you agree? How do you want to be known? As a hard worker? An honest man? Someone to be counted on? As a compassionate friend and loving husband? You can be known as all those things and more if you would wear but one title: *man of God.*

If others see you as a man after My heart, then they see you as one with a nearly impeccable reputation. I said *nearly* because you will never be perfect until you look upon My face in paradise. Until that great day, I will help you be a man of God on earth—a man whose great reputation will honor and bring glory to My name.

Joyfully,

Your Father in Heaven

> We are not peddlers of God's word like so many; but in Christ we speak as persons of sincerity, as persons sent from God and standing in his presence.
> 2 CORINTHIANS 2:17 NRSV

They couldn't argue with Stephen because he spoke with the wisdom that the Spirit had given him.

ACTS 6:10 GOD'S WORD

When he came and saw the grace of God, he rejoiced, and he exhorted them all to remain faithful to the Lord with steadfast devotion; for he was a good man, full of the Holy Spirit and of faith. And a great many people were brought to the Lord.

ACTS 11:23-24 NRSV

Do not let anyone treat you as if you are unimportant because you are young. Instead, be an example to the believers with your words, your actions, your love, your faith, and your pure life.

1 TIMOTHY 4:12 NCV

Just as you received Christ Jesus as Lord, continue to live in him, rooted and built up in him, strengthened in the faith as you were taught, and overflowing with thankfulness.

COLOSSIANS 2:6-7 NIV

Faith

Faith

Without faith no one can please God. We must believe that God is real and that he rewards everyone who searches for him.
HEBREWS 11:6 CEV

A person who is pure of heart sees goodness and purity in everything; but a person whose own heart is evil and untrusting finds evil in everything, for his dirty mind and rebellious heart color all he sees and hears.
TITUS 1:15 TLB

Thou, O man of God, flee these things; and follow after righteousness, godliness, faith, love, patience, meekness. Fight the good fight of faith, lay hold on eternal life, whereunto thou art also called, and hast professed a good profession before many witnesses.
1 TIMOTHY 6:11-12

Let us draw near with a sincere heart in full assurance of faith, having our hearts sprinkled *clean* from an evil conscience and our bodies washed with pure water.
HEBREWS 10:22 NASB

Cling tightly to your faith in Christ, and always keep your conscience clear. For some people have deliberately violated their consciences; as a result, their faith has been shipwrecked.
1 TIMOTHY 1:19 NLT

Be strong in the Lord and in his great
power. Put on the full armor of God so that
you can fight against the devil's evil tricks.
Our fight is not against people on earth but
against the rulers and authorities and the
powers of this world's darkness,
against the spiritual powers of evil
in the heavenly world.

EPHESIANS 6:10-12 NCV

Live in such a way that you are a credit to
the Message of Christ. Let nothing in your
conduct hang on whether I come or not.
Your conduct must be the same whether I
show up to see things for myself or
hear of it from a distance.

PHILIPPIANS 1:27 THE MESSAGE

After removing Saul, he made David their
king. He testified concerning him: "I have
found David son of Jesse a man after my
own heart; he will do everything
I want him to do."

ACTS 13:22 NIV

A Man of God

I Made You

You are a work of art.

My Masterpiece,

I know how you like to go outside at night and gaze up at the stars; how majestic mountains take your breath away; and how the sun setting over the ocean thrills your heart. I'm glad you love My universe so much. But now consider a much more precious design than all of these things: you!

Not only are you My most prized creation, but I had you in mind all along while I was forming this universe. I made you in My image so we could have a relationship with each other. I formed your mind so you could think; I gave you words so you could speak; and I gave you a heart so you could dream. You are My own, the one I love so much and of whom I am so proud.

With love for eternity,

Your Creator

Let the Spirit change your way of thinking and make you into a new person. You were created to be like God, and so you must please him and be truly holy.

EPHESIANS 4:23-24 CEV

*Are we not all children of the same
Father? Are we not all created by
the same God? Then why are we
faithless to each other, violating
the covenant of our ancestors?*

MALACHI 2:10 NLT

You are the one who put me together
inside my mother's body,
and I praise you because of the
wonderful way you created me.
Everything you do is marvelous!
Of this I have no doubt.

PSALM 139:13-14 CEV

Christ himself is the Creator who made
everything in heaven and earth, the things we
can see and the things we can't; the spirit
world with its kings and kingdoms, its rulers
and authorities; all were made by Christ for his
own use and glory.

COLOSSIANS 1:16 TLB

I will say to the north, "Give them up,"
and to the south, "Do not withhold;
bring my sons from far away
and my daughters from the end of the earth—
everyone who is called by my name,
whom I created for my glory,
whom I formed and made."

ISAIAH 43:6-7 NRSV

Creation

TAKE HEART

You cannot lose with Me by your side.

Dear Precious One,

I know that some days you feel as if you are being hit from all sides. The demands of work and home can be overwhelming. You can stand strong, though, because I am your Rock and your Foundation when all else around you crumbles and shakes.

I am quick to rescue you and to lift you up. Numerous times in My Word you will read of men who called upon My name and I rescued them. So in the face of all your daily stresses, keep in mind that I have overcome this world. You have nothing to fear.

With utmost love and concern,

Your Protector

I've told you all this so that trusting me, you will be unshakable and assured, deeply at peace. In this godless world you will continue to experience difficulties. But take heart! I've conquered the world.
JOHN 16:33 THE MESSAGE

On the day I called to you,
you answered me.
You made me strong
and brave.
PSALM 138:3 NCV

Be ye strong therefore, and let not your
hands be weak: for your work
shall be rewarded.
2 CHRONICLES 15:7

Why then be downcast? Why be discouraged
and sad? Hope in God! I shall yet praise him
again. Yes, I shall again praise him for his help.
PSALM 42:5 TLB

Wait on the LORD: be of good courage, and
he shall strengthen thine heart:
wait, I say, on the LORD.
PSALM 27:14

A cheerful look brings joy to the heart,
and good news gives health to the bones.
PROVERBS 15:30 NIV

"We have the LORD our God to help us and
to fight our battles for us!" These words
greatly encouraged the people.
2 CHRONICLES 32:8 NLT

Encouragement

Encouragement

I will never forget your commandments,
for you have used them
to restore my joy and health.
PSALM 119:93 NLT

Fully believe the Truth, standing in it steadfast and
firm, strong in the Lord, convinced of the Good
News that Jesus died for you, and never shifting
from trusting him to save you. This is the wonderful
news that came to each of you and is now spreading
all over the world. And I, Paul, have the joy of
telling it to others.
COLOSSIANS 1:23 TLB

Do not be afraid of what you are about to suffer. I
tell you, the devil will put some of you in prison to
test you, and you will suffer persecution for ten
days. Be faithful, even to the point of death, and I
will give you the crown of life.
REVELATION 2:10 NIV

You will experience for yourselves the truth,
and the truth will free you.
JOHN 8:32 THE MESSAGE

You should continue on as you were
when God called you.
1 CORINTHIANS 7:20 NLT

Samuel spoke to all the house of Israel, saying, "If you return to the LORD with all your heart, remove the foreign gods and the Ashtaroth from among you and direct your hearts to the LORD and serve Him alone; and He will deliver you from the hand of the Philistines."
I SAMUEL 7:3 NASB

We desire that each one of you show the same diligence so as to realize the full assurance of hope until the end, so that you will not be sluggish, but imitators of those who through faith and patience inherit the promises.
HEBREWS 6:11-12 NASB

He is a rock.
What he does is perfect,
All his ways are fair.
He is a faithful God, who does no wrong.
He is honorable and reliable.
DEUTERONOMY 32:4 GOD'S WORD

Godliness helps people all through life, while the evil are destroyed by their wickedness.
PROVERBS 13:6 NLT

Take Heart

A PASSIONATE MARRIAGE

Take pleasure in your wife.

Dear Son,

If someone were to ask you what are your top ten favorite creations, would you be honest and list "woman" as one of your answers? I know that you would want to, but I also know that you would feel awkward saying it, afraid of what people might think.

I created woman, and I want you to rejoice in her beauty. In fact, one thing many people seem to have forgotten is that I created sex. I want you to build an intimate relationship with your wife. Song of Solomon, the book of the Bible that is often misunderstood or dismissed altogether, is a reminder to you of the delight I expect you and your wife to take in each other.

Forever yours and your wife's,

The God of Passion

"You are like a private garden, my treasure, my bride! You are like a spring that no one else can drink from, a fountain of my own. You are like a lovely orchard bearing precious fruit, with the rarest of perfumes."
SONG OF SONGS 4:12-13 NLT

*Let him kiss me with the
kisses of his mouth —
For your love is better
than wine.*

SONG OF SOLOMON 1:2 NKJV

Husbands, go all out in your love for your
wives, exactly as Christ did for the church—a
love marked by giving, not getting. Christ's
love makes the church whole.
His words evoke her beauty.

EPHESIANS 5:25-26 THE MESSAGE

Don't you know that a man who does that
becomes part of her body? The Scriptures
say, "The two of them will be
like one person."

1 CORINTHIANS 6:16 CEV

"You are tall and slim like a palm tree, and
your breasts are like its clusters of dates. I
said, 'I will climb up into the palm tree and
take hold of its branches.' Now may your
breasts be like grape clusters, and the scent
of your breath like apples. May your kisses
be as exciting as the best wine, smooth and
sweet, flowing gently over lips and teeth."

SONG OF SONGS 7:7-9 NLT

Love for Your Wife

THE POWER OF PRAYER

Simple prayers unleash My greatness.

Dear Son,

You have heard the phrase "With God, nothing is impossible," and that is especially true when it is woven in your prayers. You cannot begin to fathom the strength prayer plays in your life every day and in the lives of those both near and dear to you as well as in the lives of others around the world.

The littlest prayer, My Word says, can move a mountain. Believe Me, I have moved many mountains—even in your life. I have never listened to an insignificant prayer from any of My children. I hang on every word spoken to me, so believe in My promises and bring all your mountains before Me.

Always waiting to answer,

Your Loving Father

We will devote ourselves to prayer
and to the ministry of the word.
ACTS 6:4 NASB

He listened!
He heard my prayer!
He paid attention to it!
PSALM 66:19 TLB

Hear my prayer, O LORD!
Listen to my cries for help!
Don't ignore my tears.
For I am your guest—
a traveler passing through,
as my ancestors were before me.
PSALM 39:12 NLT

The prayer offered in faith will make the sick person well; the Lord will raise him up. If he has sinned, he will be forgiven. Therefore confess your sins to each other and pray for each other so that you may be healed. The prayer of a righteous man is powerful and effective.
JAMES 5:15-16 NIV

Hear me when I call, O God of my righteousness: thou hast enlarged me *when I was* in distress; have mercy upon me, and hear my prayer.
PSALM 4:1

God Will Answer

I Am Building a Mansion for You

Paradise is waiting for you.

Dear Son,

No matter how good or bad life ever gets, always remember that this is not your home. You are simply living at a temporary address while your mansion in heaven is being prepared. You think you can picture what it will be like, but you will be overcome by its splendor when you arrive.

So the next time you are discouraged about all that is around you and are tired of living in your earthly body, turn your eyes to what is above and yet to come. Soon you will be with Me in paradise, and there will be much rejoicing when you arrive.

I'm waiting for you,

Your Savior

"There are many rooms in my Father's house.
I wouldn't tell you this, unless it was true. I am
going there to prepare a place for each of you.
After I have done this, I will come back and
take you with me. Then we will be together.
You know the way to where I am going."
JOHN 14:2-4 CEV

Blessed are *the poor in spirit:
for theirs is the kingdom
of heaven.*
MATTHEW 5:3

Praise be to the God and Father of our Lord
Jesus Christ! In his great mercy he has given
us new birth into a living hope through the
resurrection of Jesus Christ from the dead,
and into an inheritance that can never perish,
spoil or fade—kept in heaven for you.

1 PETER 1:3-4 NIV

Then the righteous will shine like the sun in
the kingdom of their Father. He who has
ears, let him hear.

MATTHEW 13:43 NIV

If we are God's children, we will receive
blessings from God together with Christ. But
we must suffer as Christ suffered so that we
will have glory as Christ has glory.

ROMANS 8:17 NCV

Blessed are those slaves whom the master
will find on the alert when he comes; truly I
say to you, that he will gird himself *to serve*,
and have them recline *at the table*, and will
come up and wait on them.

LUKE 12:37 NASB

Heaven

MY HELPER SENT TO YOU

He will never let you down.

Dear Son,

When you were a little boy you were intrigued by Western movies, books, and television heroes: The Lone Ranger, Wyatt Earp, Shane, and others. All of these were examples to you. They were the good guys who came to the aid of helpless townspeople or ranchers by helping them run off the bad guys, something they could not have done by themselves.

In a sense, the Holy Spirit was sent to you because I knew that the Evil One was riding into your life intent on destroying you. Satan attacks you from every direction, so you cannot possibly fend him off yourself. But the Holy Spirit will fill you up and guide you to victory over your enemy. You can count on Him.

In victory,

Your Lord

The Spirit of God whets our appetite by giving us a taste of what's ahead. He puts a little of heaven in our hearts so that we'll never settle for less.
2 CORINTHIANS 5:5 THE MESSAGE

Do you not know that your body is a temple of the Holy Spirit who is in you, whom you have from God, and that you are not your own?

1 CORINTHIANS 6:19 NASB

The Comforter, *which is* the Holy Ghost, whom the Father will send in my name, he shall teach you all things, and bring all things to your remembrance, whatsoever I have said unto you.

JOHN 14:26

God has actually given us his Spirit (not the world's spirit) so we can know the wonderful things God has freely given us. When we tell you this, we do not use words of human wisdom. We speak words given to us by the Spirit, using the Spirit's words to explain spiritual truths.

1 CORINTHIANS 2:12-13 NLT

Even though you are bad, you know how to give good things to your children. How much more your heavenly Father will give the Holy Spirit to those who ask him!

LUKE 11:13 NCV

Holy Spirit

Holy Spirit

It has pleased the Holy Spirit that you should not have a heavy load to carry, and we agree.
ACTS 15:28 NCV

It is written in the Scriptures:
"No one has ever seen this,
and no one has ever heard about it.
No one has ever imagined
what God has prepared for those who love him."
But God has shown us these things through the
Spirit. The Spirit searches out all things, even the
deep secrets of God.
1 CORINTHIANS 2:9-10 NCV

He has put his brand upon us—his mark of
ownership—and given us his Holy Spirit in our
hearts as guarantee that we belong to him, and as
the first installment of all that he is going to give us.
2 CORINTHIANS 1:22 TLB

The nations will know that I am the LORD who
sanctifies Israel, when My sanctuary is in their
midst forever.
EZEKIEL 37:28 NASB

Know ye not that ye are the temple of God, and
that the Spirit of God dwelleth in you?
1 CORINTHIANS 3:16

When the Spirit of truth comes, he will
guide you into all the truth; for he will not
speak on his own, but will speak whatever
he hears, and he will declare to you the
things that are to come. He will glorify me,
because he will take what is mine
and declare it to you.

JOHN 16:13-14 NRSV

The church throughout Judea, Galilee and
Samaria enjoyed a time of peace. It was
strengthened; and encouraged by the Holy
Spirit, it grew in numbers, living in the
fear of the Lord.

ACTS 9:31 NIV

Peter said to them, "Repent, and be baptized
every one of you in the name of Jesus Christ
so that your sins may be forgiven; and you
will receive the gift of the Holy Spirit."

ACTS 2:38 NRSV

You sent your good Spirit to instruct them,
and you did not stop giving them bread from
heaven or water for their thirst.

NEHEMIAH 9:20 NLT

My Helper
Sent to You

HONOR YOUR MARRIAGE VOWS

Love her as I love the church.

Dear Child,

Think back to your wedding day, My son. What a day! You were exhilarated as you and your bride embarked on this exciting adventure. There was so much to comprehend that day that it is hard now for you to recall all the details. But if you remember only one thing, remember your wedding vows.

Most people only remember the "till death us do part" phrase, but that is not the most important. Never forget the part where you promised to always love your wife.

I love you unconditionally and with a devotion that never wavers. You are to love your wife in the same way, and if you do, your marriage will definitely last a lifetime.

With abounding love,

The Author of Your Marriage

For this reason a man shall leave his father and mother and be joined to his wife, and the two shall become one flesh.
MATTHEW 19:5 NRSV

Let thy fountain be blessed:
and rejoice with the wife
of thy youth.

PROVERBS 5:18

The LORD God said, "It is not good for the
man to be alone; I will make him a helper
suitable for him."

GENESIS 2:18 NASB

Your wife will be like a fruitful vine
within your house;
your children will be like olive shoots
around your table.
Thus shall the man be blessed
who fears the LORD.

PSALM 128:3-4 NRSV

A father can give his sons homes and riches,
but only the Lord can give them
understanding wives.

PROVERBS 19:14 TLB

Enjoy life with the woman whom you love all
the days of your fleeting life which He has
given to you under the sun; for this is your
reward in life and in your toil in which you
have labored under the sun.

ECCLESIASTES 9:9 NASB

Marriage

Marriage

Give honor to marriage, and remain faithful to one another in marriage. God will surely judge people who are immoral and those who commit adultery.

HEBREWS 13:4 NLT

A capable wife who can find?
She is far more precious than jewels.

PROVERBS 31:10 NRSV

A spiritual leader must have a good reputation. He must have only one wife and have children who are believers. His children shouldn't be known for having wild lifestyles or being rebellious.

TITUS 1:6 GOD'S WORD

One of the seven angels who had the seven bowls full of the seven last plagues came and said to me, "Come, I will show you the bride, the wife of the Lamb."

REVELATION 21:9 NIV

"A man shall leave his father and mother and be joined to his wife, and the two shall become one flesh." This is a great mystery, but I speak concerning Christ and the church. Nevertheless let each one of you in particular so love his own wife as himself, and let the wife see that she respects her husband.

EPHESIANS 5:31-33 NKJV

A wife belongs to her husband instead of to herself, and a husband belongs to his wife instead of to himself.

1 CORINTHIANS 7:4 CEV

You husbands should live with your wives in an understanding way, since they are weaker than you. But show them respect, because God gives them the same blessing he gives you—the grace that gives true life. Do this so that nothing will stop your prayers.

1 PETER 3:7 NCV

A pastor must be a good man whose life cannot be spoken against. He must have only one wife, and he must be hard working and thoughtful, orderly, and full of good deeds. He must enjoy having guests in his home, and must be a good Bible teacher.

1 TIMOTHY 3:2 TLB

"For this reason a man shall leave his father and mother and be joined to his wife, and the two shall become one flesh." So they are no longer two, but one flesh. Therefore what God has joined together, let no one separate.

MARK 10:7-9 NRSV

Honor Your Marriage Vows

Rest for Your Weary Soul

Remember Me when life exhausts you.

Dear Weary One,

It's important for everyone to take a breather from the demands of life. Sometimes rest may be for your muscles, while at other times it may be for your mind or even for your soul.

No major professional sports league has a yearlong season—those fine-tuned athletes need to take a break. If they didn't have one, their skill levels would diminish, they would risk greater injuries, and they would probably burn out.

Jesus and His disciples frequently retreated from the crowds to seek a quiet place so they could be refreshed. You, too, need to take time out, because I want you to be at the top of your game in life. You who are weary come, and I will give you rest.

With assurance,

The God Who Makes All Things New

> He said, My presence shall go *with thee*,
> and I will give thee rest.
> EXODUS 33:14

The peace of God, which surpasses all comprehension, will guard your hearts and your minds in Christ Jesus.

PHILIPPIANS 4:7 NASB

"The Lord your God is with you," he declared. "He has given you peace with the surrounding nations, for I have conquered them in the name of the LORD and for his people."

1 CHRONICLES 22:18 TLB

You will have a son who will be a man of peace and rest, and I will give him rest from all his enemies on every side. His name will be Solomon, and I will grant Israel peace and quiet during his reign.

1 CHRONICLES 22:9 NIV

May the Master of Peace himself give you the gift of getting along with each other at all times, in all ways. May the Master be truly among you!

2 THESSALONIANS 3:16 THE MESSAGE

I will listen to what God the LORD will say; he promises peace to his people, his saints— but let them not return to folly.

PSALM 85:8 NIV

Rest

Rest

I said, Oh that I had wings like a dove! for then
would I fly away, and be at rest.
PSALM 55:6

"Are you tired? Worn out? Burned out on religion?
Come to me. Get away with me and you'll recover
your life. I'll show you how to take a real rest. Walk
with me and work with me—watch how I do it.
Learn the unforced rhythms of grace. I won't lay
anything heavy or ill-fitting on you. Keep company
with me and you'll learn to live freely and lightly."
MATTHEW 11:28-29 THE MESSAGE

Who among you fears the LORD
and obeys his servant?
That person may walk in the dark and have no light.
Then let him trust in the LORD
and depend on his God.
ISAIAH 50:10 NCV

After all it is *only* just for God to repay with
affliction those who afflict you, and *to give* relief to
you who are afflicted and to us as well when the
Lord Jesus will be revealed from heaven with His
mighty angels in flaming fire.
2 THESSALONIANS 1:6-7 NASB

Discipline your children, and they will give you rest;
they will give delight to your heart.
PROVERBS 29:17 NRSV

You will be secure, because there is hope;
you will look about you and take your
rest in safety.

JOB 11:18 NIV

When you cross over the Jordan and live in
the land that the LORD your God is allotting
to you, and when he gives you rest from your
enemies all around so that you live in safety.

DEUTERONOMY 12:10 NRSV

Thus says the high and exalted One
Who lives forever, whose name is Holy,
"I dwell *on* a high and holy place,
And *also* with the contrite and lowly of spirit
In order to revive the spirit of the lowly
And to revive the heart of the contrite."

ISAIAH 57:15 NASB

He said to them, "Come aside by yourselves
to a deserted place and rest a while." For
there were many coming and going, and they
did not even have time to eat.

MARK 6:31 NKJV

Rest for Your
Weary Soul

TRUE WEALTH

Be content at all times.

Dear Child of Mine,

As you go to work this week, consider what makes a man rich. Is it a six-figure income, designer suits from Italy, a fully-equipped SUV, a 5,000-square-foot house and beachfront vacation getaway? There's nothing wrong with any of these material possessions, but a rich man they do not make. There's only one way to assess whether you are wealthy, and that is to stop and ask yourself one question: Am I content?

You see, if the wealthiest man in the world is not content, then he is a poor man indeed, and his heart will be miserable the rest of his days. But if the poorest of the poor is content, then he is truly rich and will forever be blessed.

With wealth that no money can buy,

The God Who Richly Blesses

> Serving God does make us very rich, if we are satisfied with what we have.
>
> 1 TIMOTHY 6:6 NCV

*Not that I was ever in need,
for I have learned how to
get along happily whether I
have much or little.*

PHILIPPIANS 4:11 TLB

It is better to live right and be poor
than to be sinful and rich.

PSALM 37:16 CEV

Keep falsehood and lies far from me;
give me neither poverty nor riches,
but give me only my daily bread.

PROVERBS 30:8 NIV

Stay away from the love of money; be
satisfied with what you have. For God has
said, "I will never, *never* fail you
nor forsake you."

HEBREWS 13:5 TLB

You didn't choose me! I chose you! I
appointed you to go and produce lovely fruit
always, so that no matter what you ask for
from the Father, using my name,
he will give it to you.

JOHN 15:16 TLB

Contentment

LEAN FULLY ON ME

My shoulders are broad and strong.

Dear Son,

In a world of recovery programs, self-help books, and motivational speakers, it's easy to forget that I am greater than all those solutions. When it comes to renewing, encouraging, uplifting, strengthening, and motivating your body and soul, no one can do that better than I can.

Only I am strong enough to support the full weight of your problems and challenges. I will never grow weary from carrying your burdens; in fact, I love it when you put your arm over My shoulder and we walk together. The more you turn to Me and rely on My strength, the more you will accomplish great things.

Always with strength for the day,

Your Heavenly Father

Every morning tell him, "Thank you for your kindness," and every evening rejoice in all his faithfulness.
PSALM 92:2 TLB

Your lovingkindness, O LORD,
extends to the heavens,
Your faithfulness reaches
to the skies.
PSALM 36:5 NASB

O LORD, You *are* my God.
I will exalt You,
I will praise Your name,
For You have done wonderful *things*;
Your counsels of old *are* faithfulness *and* truth.
ISAIAH 25:1 NKJV

I do not hide your righteousness in my heart;
I speak of your faithfulness and salvation.
I do not conceal your love and your truth
from the great assembly.
PSALM 40:10 NIV

Will your love be told in the grave?
Will your loyalty be told in the place of death?
PSALM 88:11 NCV

When we were utterly helpless with no way of
escape, Christ came at just the right time and
died for us sinners who had no use for him.
ROMANS 5:6 TLB

Faithfulness of God

Faithfulness of God

I know, O LORD, that your decisions are fair;
you disciplined me because I needed it.
Now let your unfailing love comfort me,
just as you promised me, your servant.
PSALM 119:75-76 NLT

Righteousness will be his belt
and faithfulness the sash around his waist.
ISAIAH 11:5 NIV

Sarah, too, had faith, and because of this she was
able to become a mother in spite of her old age, for
she realized that God, who gave her his promise,
would certainly do what he said.
HEBREWS 11:11 TLB

The steadfast love of the LORD never ceases,
his mercies never come to an end;
they are new every morning;
great is your faithfulness.
LAMENTATIONS 3:22-23 NRSV

If we confess our sins, he is faithful and just
and will forgive us our sins and purify us
from all unrighteousness.
1 JOHN 1:9 NIV

The Lord is faithful, who will establish you and
guard *you* from the evil one.
2 THESSALONIANS 3:3 NKJV

We are afflicted in every way, but not crushed; perplexed, but not despairing; persecuted, but not forsaken; struck down, but not destroyed.

2 CORINTHIANS 4:8-9 NASB

Faithful is He who calls you, and He also will bring it to pass.

1 THESSALONIANS 5:24 NASB

I will sing of your steadfast love,
O LORD, forever;
with my mouth I will proclaim your
faithfulness to all generations.

PSALM 89:1 NRSV

If you find life difficult because you're doing what God said, take it in stride. Trust him. He knows what he's doing, and he'll keep on doing it.

1 PETER 4:19 THE MESSAGE

The LORD loves justice and
will not leave those who worship him.
He will always protect them,
but the children of
the wicked will die.

PSALM 37:28 NCV

Lean Fully
on Me

MADE TO SERVE

You were created for a purpose.

My Own,

Think of the work of a master potter. Now consider his handiwork and its intended use. It is not only beautiful, as he hoped it would be, but it was made for a specific purpose. What good is a decanter that is never used to pour out cool, thirst-quenching water for one who is parched?

I have molded and shaped you. When I created you, I knew in My heart and My mind what I wanted the finished piece to look like. You are a spectacular work of art, My son, but you are much more than that. You are a vessel—you are My servant— intended to pour out My refreshing goodness to a thirsting world.

Your Lord and King,

The Only Source of Living Water

Respect the LORD your God and serve him. Be loyal
to him and make your promises in his name.
DEUTERONOMY 10:20 NCV

Each one should use whatever gift he has received to serve others, faithfully administering God's grace in its various forms.

1 PETER 4:10 NIV

Now fear the LORD and serve him with all faithfulness. Throw away the gods your forefathers worshiped beyond the River and in Egypt, and serve the LORD.

JOSHUA 24:14 NIV

Look at Apollos and me as mere servants of Christ who have been put in charge of explaining God's secrets.

1 CORINTHIANS 4:1 NLT

So now, O Israel, what does the LORD your God require of you? Only to fear the LORD your God, to walk in all his ways, to love him, to serve the LORD your God with all your heart and with all your soul.

DEUTERONOMY 10:12 NRSV

It shall come to pass, if ye shall hearken diligently unto my commandments which I command you this day, to love the LORD your God, and to serve him with all your heart and with all your soul.

DEUTERONOMY 11:13

Serving

TRUE LOVE

Show others how much you care.

Dear Beloved,

It's hard for many men to show love to others. To them it seems to diminish their masculinity or jeopardize their status in the business world. But I'm not talking about hugging everybody with whom you work or telling them that you love them. There are so many other ways you can show love for your fellow man.

Let someone merge in front of you on the highway—even if that person didn't use a turn signal. Listen attentively when someone is talking. Smile a little more. Get your colleague a cup of coffee. Praise someone's efforts. All these and other little gestures let My love shine through you—all while keeping intact your reputation of being a man's man.

Forever yours,

The Lord God

CONTINUE TO LOVE each other with true brotherly love.
HEBREWS 13:1 TLB

These three remain: faith, hope and love. But the greatest of these is love.
1 CORINTHIANS 13:13 NIV

The second command is this: "Love your neighbor as you love yourself." There are no commands more important than these.
MARK 12:31 NCV

You can't go wrong when you love others. When you add up everything in the law code, the sum total is *love*.
ROMANS 13:10 THE MESSAGE

This is My commandment, that you love one another, just as I have loved you. Greater love has no one than this, that one lay down his life for his friends.
JOHN 15:12-13 NASB

If *there be* therefore any consolation in Christ, if any comfort of love, if any fellowship of the Spirit, if any bowels and mercies, Fulfil ye my joy, that ye be like-minded, having the same love, *being* of one accord, of one mind.
PHILIPPIANS 2:1-2

Love for Others

Love for Others

*Ointment and perfume rejoice the heart: so doth
the sweetness of a man's friend by hearty counsel.*
PROVERBS 27:9

By this all will know that you are My disciples,
if you have love for one another.
JOHN 13:35 NKJV

Listen, all of you. Love your *enemies.* Do *good* to
those who *hate* you.
LUKE 6:27 TLB

Thou shalt not avenge, nor bear any grudge against
the children of thy people, but thou shalt love thy
neighbour as thyself: I *am* the LORD.
LEVITICUS 19:18

There is no fear in love. But perfect love drives out
fear, because fear has to do with punishment. The
one who fears is not made perfect in love.
1 JOHN 4:18 NIV

We have come to know and have believed the love
which God has for us. God is love, and the one who
abides in love abides in God, and God abides in him.
1 JOHN 4:16 NASB

Love sincerely. Hate evil. Hold on to what is good. Be devoted to each other like a loving family. Excel in showing respect for each other.
ROMANS 12:9-10 GOD'S WORD

Show respect for everyone. Love your Christian brothers and sisters. Fear God. Show respect for the king.
1 PETER 2:17 NLT

He that loveth not knoweth not God; for God is love.
1 JOHN 4:8

A bowl of soup with someone you love is better than steak with someone you hate.
PROVERBS 15:17 NLT

In this is love, not that we loved God but that he loved us and sent his Son to be the atoning sacrifice for our sins.
1 JOHN 4:10 NRSV

I am giving you these commands so that you may love one another.
JOHN 15:17 NRSV

True Love

STRENGTH IN TIMES OF WEAKNESS

I will rescue you with power and might.

My Own,

When the world seems to crash down on you, don't try supporting it on your own. Allow Me to come to your aid. I will not only protect you from everything that is falling on you, but I will clear the resulting debris that surrounds you and make a path for you to carry on.

So when you face trials at work, come to Me. When your family goes through a time of crisis, call My name. When tragedy strikes a loved one, expect My powerful, loving arms to surround you. Let Me overwhelm you with My strength so that your faith can be a witness to others.

With overwhelming strength,

Almighty God

> The LORD is my strength and song,
> And He has become my salvation.
> PSALM 118:14 NASB

You alone are God!
Only you are a mighty rock.
You are my strong fortress,
and you set me free.
2 SAMUEL 22:32-33 CEV

Sing for joy to God, our strength;
shout out loud to the God of Jacob.
PSALM 81:1 NCV

The LORD is my strength and my might,
and he has become my salvation;
this is my God, and I will praise him,
my father's God, and I will exalt him.
EXODUS 15:2 NRSV

You are awesome, O God, in your sanctuary;
the God of Israel gives power and strength to
his people. Praise be to God!
PSALM 68:35 NIV

You have been a strength to the poor,
A strength to the needy in his distress,
A refuge from the storm,
A shade from the heat;
For the blast of the terrible ones *is* as a
storm *against* the wall.
ISAIAH 25:4 NKJV

Strength

Live Victoriously

In Me you can achieve anything.

Dear Son,

Remember the first time you rode your bike by yourself—without the training wheels? With help at your side, you started pedaling. Your handle bars were a little wobbly and your knees much more so. Then, in a split second, you went from fearful to courageous and pulled away from the person who had been holding you up. You had done it! You had finally pulled off what was impossible just seconds before.

Now translate that into your present life. I am running beside you, holding you up, encouraging you. Your mind is racing, telling you that you can't do this or can't do that. But then you are filled with My strength, and you pull away, riding on to victory.

In power and strength,

The Almighty

COME, EVERYONE, AND clap for joy! Shout triumphant praises to the Lord!
PSALM 47:1 TLB

*God rules the nations
from his sacred throne.*
PSALM 47:8 CEV

Sing to the LORD a new song,
because he has done miracles.
By his right hand and holy arm
he has won the victory.
PSALM 98:1 NCV

I thank God, who always leads us in victory
because of Christ. Wherever we go, God
uses us to make clear what it means to know
Christ. It's like a fragrance that fills the air.
2 CORINTHIANS 2:14 GOD'S WORD

For thou, LORD, hast made me glad through
thy work: I will triumph in the
works of thy hands.
PSALM 92:4

I saw God before me for all time.
Nothing can shake me; he's right by my side.
I'm glad from the inside out, ecstatic;
I've pitched my tent in the land of hope.
ACTS 2:25-26 THE MESSAGE

Victory

Victory

Having disarmed the powers and authorities,
he made a public spectacle of them,
triumphing over them by the cross.
COLOSSIANS 2:15 NIV

Yours, O LORD, is the greatness and the power and
the glory and the victory and the majesty, indeed
everything that is in the heavens and the earth;
Yours is the dominion, O LORD, and You exalt
Yourself as head over all.
1 CHRONICLES 29:11 NASB

The sting of death *is* sin, and the strength of sin *is*
the law. But thanks *be* to God, who gives us the
victory through our Lord Jesus Christ.
1 CORINTHIANS 15:56-57 NKJV

He defeated nations for us
and put them under our control.
PSALM 47:3 NCV

He will not break a crushed blade of grass
or put out even a weak flame
until he makes justice win the victory.
MATTHEW 12:20 NCV

He will swallow up death forever! The
Sovereign LORD will wipe away all tears. He
will remove forever all insults and mockery
against his land and people.
The LORD has spoken!

ISAIAH 25:8 NLT

So, my dear brothers, since future victory is
sure, be strong and steady, always abounding
in the Lord's work, for you know that nothing
you do for the Lord is ever wasted as it would
be if there were no resurrection.

I CORINTHIANS 15:58 TLB

Moses and the Israelites sang this song in
praise of the LORD:
I sing praises to the LORD for his great victory!
He has thrown the horses
and their riders into the sea.

EXODUS 15:1 CEV

When this corruptible has put on
incorruption, and this mortal has put on
immortality, then shall be brought to pass the
saying that is written: *"Death is
swallowed up in victory."*

I CORINTHIANS 15:54 NKJV

Live Victoriously

THE BEST IS YET TO COME

It won't be long now.

Dear Son,

The next time you are standing on the beach, looking at powerful ocean waves crash upon the shore, remember . . . When you climb atop a majestic mountain and look around for miles at the surrounding timberline, remember . . . When you hear a piece of music that stirs your soul, remember . . . And when you hear a young child giggling uncontrollably, remember . . .

In the midst of pain and suffering, trials and tribulations, there are many good things—no, wonderful things—that I have created on earth for you. But remember this: the best is yet to come. Nothing on this earth will hold a flame to the glory that awaits you in heaven. Always remember.

Joyfully,

Your Father in Heaven

His unchanging plan has always been to adopt
us into his own family by bringing us to himself
through Jesus Christ. And this gave
him great pleasure.
EPHESIANS 1:5 NLT

I have not yet reached my goal, and I am not perfect. But Christ has taken hold of me. So I keep on running and struggling to take hold of the prize.

PHILIPPIANS 3:12 CEV

I endure all things for the elect's sakes, that they may also obtain the salvation which is in Christ Jesus with eternal glory. *It is* a faithful saying: For if we be dead with *him*, we shall also live with *him*.

2 TIMOTHY 2:10-11

Thomas said, "Lord, we don't even know where you are going! How can we know the way?" "I am the way, the truth, and the life!" Jesus answered. "Without me, no one can go to the Father."

JOHN 14:5-6 CEV

For the Lord Himself will descend from heaven with a shout, with the voice of an archangel, and with the trumpet of God. And the dead in Christ will rise first. Then we who are alive and remain shall be caught up together with them in the clouds to meet the Lord in the air. And thus we shall always be with the Lord. Therefore comfort one another with these words.

1 THESSALONIANS 4:16-18 NKJV

Future

TALK TO ME; I AM LISTENING

I promise that I will always hear you.

Dear Son,

How I long for you to be in communion with Me. I cherish every minute that you spend with Me pouring out your heart. As you have discovered over and over, there is no one on earth who knows you inside and out as I do. Before you even open your mouth to talk to Me, I have already heard the longings of your heart.

Do not hesitate to come to Me for anything. Nothing is too great or too small for Me. Do not be afraid to tell Me anything. I want to hear everything you are feeling. Whenever you come to Me, I will already be there waiting to listen to you and to share My love with you.

With loving, open arms,

Your Father

The LORD has heard my cry for help;
the LORD will answer my prayer.
PSALM 6:9 NCV

Everyone who asks, receives.
Everyone who seeks, finds.
And the door is opened to
everyone who knocks.
LUKE 11:10 NLT

Moses and Aaron were among his priests,
Samuel was among those
who called on his name;
they called on the LORD
and he answered them.
PSALM 99:6 NIV

My voice You shall hear
in the morning, O LORD;
In the morning I will direct *it* to You,
And I will look up.
PSALM 5:3 NKJV

It was at this time that He went off to the
mountain to pray, and He spent the
whole night in prayer to God.
LUKE 6:12 NASB

The Lord's eyes are on those
who do what he approves.
His ears hear their prayer.
The Lord confronts those who do evil.
1 PETER 3:12 GOD'S WORD

Prayer

FEED MY SHEEP

Take care of My own.

Dear Loved One,

Look at all the people around you. You would never know it, but they need you. They need who you are, what you know, and to know how much more of an impact I can have on their lives. They are hungry for the Truth that is Me.

That is why you should take Me seriously when I tell you to feed My sheep, because no one else besides you can make the same impact on them. If you were hired to take care of real sheep, it would be vital to the sheep's health that you guide them to fresh grass so they could eat. As My servant, I want you to look after My sheep and guide them every day in just the same way.

With loving care,

Your Good Shepherd

> You then, my child, be strong in the grace that is in Christ Jesus; and what you have heard from me through many witnesses entrust to faithful people who will be able to teach others as well.
> 2 TIMOTHY 2:1-2 NRSV

*Let us aim for harmony
in the church and try to build
each other up.*
ROMANS 14:19 NLT

He said to him the third time, "Simon son of
John, do you love me?" Peter felt hurt
because he said to him the third time, "Do
you love me?" And he said to him, "Lord, you
know everything; you know that I love you."
Jesus said to him, "Feed my sheep."
JOHN 21:17 NRSV

Now may the God of peace, who brought
again from the dead our Lord Jesus, equip
you with all you need for doing his will. May
he who became the great Shepherd of the
sheep by an everlasting agreement between
God and you, signed with his blood, produce
in you through the power of Christ
all that is pleasing to him. To him be
glory forever and ever.
HEBREWS 13:20-21 TLB

LET LOVE BE your greatest aim; nevertheless,
ask also for the special abilities the Holy Spirit
gives, and especially the gift of prophecy,
being able to preach the messages of God.
I CORINTHIANS 14:1 TLB

Discipleship

TRUE SUCCESS

You can succeed in anything.

Dear One,

What do you think of when you hear the word *success*? A six-figure income? An impressive title behind your name? A nice house and a new car? Maybe you think of athletes who have won championships and played in all-star games. Or perhaps success can be seen in the relationships you have with your family and other friends.

There's nothing wrong with any of those pictures you have formed in your mind. They are all good, and they are all, in essence, glimpses of earthly successes. But when you think about success, don't leave Me out of the equation. I want you to be successful, and I want you to win in life. And with Me, you will be more successful than you could ever imagine.

Always pulling for you,

Your Great Encourager

> His master saw that the LORD was with him,
> and that the LORD caused all that he did to
> prosper in his hands.
> GENESIS 39:3 NRSV

*Pray for the peace of
Jerusalem:
"May they prosper
who love you."*
PSALM 122:6 NKJV

He is like a tree planted beside streams—
a tree that produces fruit in season
and whose leaves do not wither.
He succeeds in everything he does.
PSALM 1:3 GOD'S WORD

Now, my son, the LORD be with you, so that you
may succeed in building the house of the LORD
your God, as he has spoken concerning you.
1 CHRONICLES 22:11 NRSV

Early the next morning, as everyone got ready to
leave for the desert near Tekoa, Jehoshaphat
stood up and said, "Listen my friends, if we trust
the LORD God and believe what these prophets
have told us, the LORD will help us,
and we will be successful."
2 CHRONICLES 20:20 CEV

That is why, for Christ's sake, I delight in
weaknesses, in insults, in hardships, in
persecutions, in difficulties. For when I am weak,
then I am strong.
2 CORINTHIANS 12:10 NIV

Success

Success

It is the blessing of the LORD that makes rich,
And He adds no sorrow to it.
PROVERBS 10:22 NASB

The trustworthy will get a rich reward. But the
person who wants to get rich quick
will only get into trouble.
PROVERBS 28:20 NLT

Solomon finished the Temple of the LORD and his
royal palace. He had success in doing everything
he planned in the Temple of the LORD
and his own palace.
2 CHRONICLES 7:11 NCV

God, whom I serve with my spirit by announcing
the gospel of his Son, is my witness that without
ceasing I remember you always in my prayers, asking
that by God's will I may somehow at last
succeed in coming to you.
ROMANS 1:9-10 NRSV

You will have God's blessing,
as you plant your crops beside streams,
while your donkeys and cattle roam freely about.
ISAIAH 32:20 CEV

We're the best of friends, and I pray for good
fortune in everything you do, and for your good
health—that your everyday affairs prosper,
as well as your soul!

3 JOHN 2 THE MESSAGE

I am sowing peace and prosperity among you.
Your crops will prosper; the grapevines will be
weighted down with fruit; the ground will be
fertile, with plenty of rain; all these blessings will
be given to the people left in the land.

ZECHARIAH 8:12 TLB

If you willingly obey me,
the best crops in the land will be yours.
But if you turn against me,
your enemies will kill you.
I, the LORD, have spoken.

ISAIAH 1:19-20 CEV

The truly happy people are those who carefully
study God's perfect law that makes people free,
and they continue to study it. They do not forget
what they heard, but they obey what God's
teaching says. Those who do this
will be made happy.

JAMES 1:25 NCV

True Success

MAKING TOUGH DECISIONS

You don't have to go it alone.

Oh, Perplexed One,

Every day you are faced with many decisions. Some of them are little decisions: paper or plastic, regular or decaffeinated, brown shoes or black, highway or side streets, and so forth. I'm interested in every part of your life, but do you think of Me when making these choices?

What about the bigger decisions in life? Find a new job or stay put? Buy a new car or fix up the old one? Follow the crowd or stand alone? You know that you don't have to make these decisions on your own. I'm willing and waiting to help. All you need to do is call on Me; I will guide you and help you choose wisely.

Your best choice is seeking Me first,

The All-Knowing God

> Those who obey him will not be punished.
> The wise man will find a time
> and a way to do what he says.
> ECCLESIASTES 8:5 TLB

Solid food is for the mature,
who because of practice have
their senses trained to
discern good and evil.
HEBREWS 5:14 NASB

God said: Solomon, I'm pleased that you asked for this. You could have asked to live a long time or to be rich. Or you could have asked for your enemies to be destroyed. Instead, you asked for wisdom to make right decisions. So I'll make you wiser than anyone who has ever lived or ever will live.
1 KINGS 3:10-12 CEV

The natural man does not receive the things of the Spirit of God; for they are foolishness to him; nor can he know *them,* because they are spiritually discerned.
1 CORINTHIANS 2:14 NKJV

He gives one person the power to perform miracles, and to another the ability to prophesy. He gives someone else the ability to know whether it is really the Spirit of God or another spirit that is speaking. Still another person is given the ability to speak in unknown languages, and another is given the ability to interpret what is being said.
1 CORINTHIANS 12:10 NLT

Discernment

Know That I Am God

There is no substitute for My power.

Dear Son,

Do you know who I am? Who I really am? I am not just a god—I am *the* God. The Alpha and the Omega. I have always existed, and I always will. Others may lead you to believe that I simply made the universe and am just sitting back watching it run its course. That's not true.

I flooded the earth and restored it. I led the Israelites out of slavery and to the Promised Land. I was with Daniel in the lions' den, I never gave up on My servant Job, and I sacrificed My only Son so that you could be saved.

Don't let anyone tell you otherwise. I am almighty God, and you can always count on Me!

With all power and might,

God

Praise the LORD our God,
and worship at the Temple,
his footstool. He is holy.
PSALM 99:5 NCV

Don't you dare
tempt the Lord
your God.
LUKE 4:8 THE MESSAGE

Bravo, GOD, bravo!
Gods and all angels shout, "Encore!"
In awe before the glory,
in awe before God's visible power.
Stand at attention!
Dress your best to honor him!
PSALM 29:1-2 THE MESSAGE

I'm sure you have heard about the Good
News for the people of Israel—that there is
peace with God through Jesus, the Messiah,
who is Lord of all creation.
ACTS 10:36 TLB

At this I fell at his feet to worship him. But he
said to me, "Do not do it! I am a fellow-servant
with you and with your brothers who
hold to the testimony of Jesus. Worship God!
For the testimony of Jesus
is the spirit of prophecy."
REVELATION 19:10 NIV

Worship

Worship

Come, let us worship and bow down,
Let us kneel before the LORD our Maker.
PSALM 95:6 NASB

Know that the LORD is God.
It is he that made us, and we are his;
we are his people, and the sheep of his pasture.
Enter his gates with thanksgiving,
and his courts with praise.
Give thanks to him, bless his name.
PSALM 100:3-4 NRSV

Be silent, all mankind, before the Lord, for he has
come to earth from heaven, from his holy home.
ZECHARIAH 2:13 TLB

Be still, and know that I am God;
I will be exalted among the nations.
PSALM 46:10 NIV

The LORD your God you shall fear; him you shall
serve, and by his name alone you shall swear.
DEUTERONOMY 6:13 NRSV

I am the LORD your God; I brought you out of the
land of Egypt where you were slaves. You must not
have any other gods except me.
DEUTERONOMY 5:6-7 NCV

I am the LORD your God, who rescued you
from slavery in Egypt.
Do not worship any other gods besides me.
EXODUS 20:2-3 NLT

Go away Satan! The Scriptures say:
"Worship the Lord your God
and serve only him."
MATTHEW 4:10 CEV

The LORD, who brought you up out of the
land of Egypt with great power and a
stretched out arm, him shall ye fear, and him
shall ye worship, and to him
shall ye do sacrifice.
2 KINGS 17:36

Give to the LORD the glory he deserves!
Bring your offering
and come to worship him.
Worship the LORD in all his holy splendor.
1 CHRONICLES 16:29 NLT

We believe and know that you are
the Holy One from God.
JOHN 6:69 NCV

Know That I Am God

THE POWER OF TWO OR MORE

Come together as one.

Dear Son,

Think about trying to pull something using a single rope. You can only tug so hard before that rope breaks. Now consider taking three ropes and weaving them together. How much could you pull then? More than three times the weight, right? You would then have not only the strength of three individual ropes, but you would have the added strength of the three coming together as one.

That is My hope for you. Each man can only handle so much on his own—after all, you're only human. But imagine the possibilities when you join forces. United and fortified through Me, you can accomplish mighty things for Me.

Go forth and conquer in My name,

Your Ultimate Strength

> Just as iron sharpens iron,
> friends sharpen the minds of each other.
> PROVERBS 27:17 CEV

*In all my prayers for all of you,
I always pray with joy because
of your partnership in the
gospel from the first day
until now.*

PHILIPPIANS 1:4-5 NIV

The whole body depends on Christ, and all
the parts of the body are joined and held
together. Each part does its own work to
make the whole body grow
and be strong with love.

EPHESIANS 4:16 NCV

This is the life we have seen and heard. We
are reporting about it to you also so that you,
too, can have a relationship with us. Our
relationship is with the Father and with his
Son Jesus Christ. We are writing this so that
we can be completely filled with joy.

1 JOHN 1:3-4 GOD'S WORD

God gave me the work of telling all people
about the plan for his secret, which has been
hidden in him since the beginning of time. He
is the One who created everything.

EPHESIANS 3:9 NCV

Fellowship

Continue to Bear Fruit

Never be satisfied with where you are.

My Own,

What good is an orange tree or a cherry tree if it doesn't bear fruit? If a fruit tree doesn't produce, all you have is a nice shade tree. But shade is not the reason why you plant a fruit tree; fruit is. If, however, you cultivate that tree properly in the spring and take care of it during the winter, you will enjoy its fruit in the summer. And the older the tree, the more it grows and the more fruit it produces.

You can look at your faith in the same way that you would look at a fruit tree. If you feed your faith with consistent doses of prayer, My Word, and service, then it is sure to grow big and strong and bring forth fine fruit.

May your faith be bountiful,

The Great Gardener

Not because I desire a gift: but I desire fruit
that may abound to your account.
PHILIPPIANS 4:17

Light brings every kind of goodness, right living, and truth.

EPHESIANS 5:9 NCV

The good news is spreading all over the world with great success. It has spread in that same way among you, ever since the first day you learned the truth about God's wonderful kindness.

COLOSSIANS 1:6 CEV

As for what was sown on good soil, this is the one who hears the word and understands it, who indeed bears fruit and yields, in one case a hundredfold, in another sixty, and in another thirty.

MATTHEW 13:23 NRSV

He cuts away every branch of mine that doesn't produce fruit. But he trims clean every branch that does produce fruit, so that it will produce even more fruit.

JOHN 15:2 CEV

I do not want you to be unaware, brethren, that I often planned to come to you (but was hindered until now), that I might have some fruit among you also, just as among the other Gentiles.

ROMANS 1:13 NKJV

Growth

Growth

But the fruit of the Spirit is love, joy, peace,
patience, kindness, goodness, faithfulness,
gentleness and self-control.
Against such things there is no law.
GALATIANS 5:22-23 NIV

You give glory to my Father when you produce a
lot of fruit and therefore show that you are
my disciples.
JOHN 15:8 GOD'S WORD

God is the one who gives seed to the farmer and
then bread to eat. In the same way, he will give you
many opportunities to do good, and he will produce
a great harvest of generosity in you.
2 CORINTHIANS 9:10 NLT

If *I am* to live *on* in the flesh, this *will mean* fruitful
labor for me; and I do not know which to choose.
PHILIPPIANS 1:22 NASB

As newborn babes, desire the sincere milk of the
word, that ye may grow thereby.
1 PETER 2:2

The wisdom that comes from above is first of all
pure. Then it is peaceful, gentle, obedient, filled with
mercy and good deeds, impartial, and sincere. A
harvest that has God's approval comes from the
peace planted by peacemakers.
JAMES 3:17-18 GOD'S WORD

Grow in the grace and knowledge of our
Lord and Savior Jesus Christ. To him be
glory both now and forever! Amen.
2 PETER 3:18 NIV

You are like a building that was built on the
foundation of the apostles and prophets.
Christ Jesus himself is the most important
stone in that building, and that whole
building is joined together in Christ.
He makes it grow and become a
holy temple in the Lord.
EPHESIANS 2:20-21 NCV

We will hold to the truth in love, becoming
more and more in every way like Christ,
who is the head of his body, the church.
EPHESIANS 4:15 NLT

Dear brothers, giving thanks to God for you
is not only the right thing to do, but it is our
duty to God, because of the really wonderful
way your faith has grown, and because of
your growing love for each other.
2 THESSALONIANS 1:3 TLB

Continue to
Bear Fruit

STICKING CLOSER THAN A BROTHER

Friendship is vital to life.

Dear Beloved,

For the most part, when you were growing up you could count on your best friends to be there for you, to support you, and to be your ally in all situations. In fact, your friends were often more reliable—at least in your own eyes—than those in your family. To this day, many of those friends remain significant to you and you to them.

I never want you to lose that special bond with your friends. I brought you together so you could go through life with others who share your passions and your dreams. But even your friends may fail you at times. I am your greatest Friend, who will never let you down nor leave your side.

Always there for you,

Your Friend and Savior

There are "friends" who pretend to be friends, but there is a friend who sticks closer than a brother.
PROVERBS 18:24 TLB

*Friends love through all kinds
of weather, and families
stick together in all kinds
of trouble.*
PROVERBS 17:17
THE MESSAGE

Here is how to measure it—the greatest love
is shown when people lay down their lives for
their friends. You are my friends if you obey
me. I no longer call you servants, because a
master doesn't confide in his servants. Now
you are my friends, since I have told you
everything the Father told me.
JOHN 15:13-15 NLT

No man will *be able to* stand before you all
the days of your life. Just as I have been with
Moses, I will be with you;
I will not fail you or forsake you.
JOSHUA 1:5 NASB

The scripture was fulfilled that says,
"Abraham believed God, and it was credited
to him as righteousness,"
and he was called God's friend.
JAMES 2:23 NIV

Friendship

A PERSONAL HANDBOOK ON LIFE

The Bible is your owner's manual.

Dear Son,

I know that you've heard people joke about how life would be easier if they had been given an owner's manual when they came into this world. Well, you do have one available to you: the Bible. It covers everything you will ever encounter, and it is timeless. It spans from before time began all the way to eternity.

Ecclesiastes 1:9 says that there is nothing new under the sun, so if you search, you will find an answer. Don't let people try to convince you that the Bible is nothing more than a book of rules. It is a volume full of life. It is My gift to you, a personal letter for you to read and embrace. I hope you do just that.

Reaching out through the written Word,

The Author of Life

May I never forget your words, for they are
my only hope.
PSALM 119:43 TLB

Teach me to follow you,
and I will obey your truth.
Always keep me faithful.
PSALM 86:11 CEV

You also were included in Christ when you
heard the word of truth, the gospel of your
salvation. Having believed, you were marked
in him with a seal, the promised Holy Spirit.
EPHESIANS 1:13 NIV

Lord, to whom shall we go?
You have words of eternal life.
JOHN 6:68 NASB

You have this faith and love because of your
hope, and what you hope for is kept safe for
you in heaven.
COLOSSIANS 1:5 NCV

Let the word of Christ richly dwell within
you, with all wisdom teaching and
admonishing one another with psalms *and*
hymns *and* spiritual songs, singing with
thankfulness in your hearts to God.
COLOSSIANS 3:16 NASB

God's Word

God's Word

Preach the Word; be prepared in season and out of season; correct, rebuke and encourage — with great patience and careful instruction.

2 TIMOTHY 4:2 NIV

Now they know that everything you have given me is from you; for the words that you gave to me I have given to them, and they have received them and know in truth that I came from you; and they have believed that you sent me.

JOHN 17:7-8 NRSV

If you teach these things to other followers, you will be a good servant of Christ Jesus. You will show that you have grown up on the teachings about our faith and on the good instructions you have obeyed.

1 TIMOTHY 4:6 CEV

He must have a strong and steadfast belief in the trustworthy message he was taught; then he will be able to encourage others with right teaching and show those who oppose it where they are wrong.

TITUS 1:9 NLT

God's word is living and active. It is sharper than any two-edged sword and cuts as deep as the place where soul and spirit meet, the place where joints and marrow meet. God's Word judges a person's thoughts and intentions.

HEBREWS 4:12 GOD'S WORD

It takes more than bread to stay alive. It takes
a steady stream of words from God's mouth.

MATTHEW 4:4 THE MESSAGE

Earth and sky will be destroyed, but the
words I have said will never be destroyed.

MATTHEW 24:35 NCV

He humbled you by letting you hunger, then
by feeding you with manna, with which neither
you nor your ancestors were acquainted, in
order to make you understand that one does
not live by bread alone, but by every word
that comes from the mouth of the LORD.

DEUTERONOMY 8:3 NRSV

"This message is near you. It's in your mouth
and in your heart." This is the message
of faith that we spread.

ROMANS 10:8 GOD'S WORD

We have faithfully preached the truth.
God's power has been working in us. We
have righteousness as our weapon, both to
attack and to defend ourselves.

2 CORINTHIANS 6:7 NLT

A Personal
Handbook on Life

SET YOUR SIGHTS HIGH

Don't be afraid to dream big.

Dear Son,

Go ahead and set goals that may seem unfeasible to you. You will be more than pleasantly surprised, because what you think is impossible is attainable through me. A baseball team that hasn't been to the World Series in nearly one hundred years still begins each season at the same place every other team does: 0-0, with its sights set on participating in that classic October series.

If you don't expect to succeed, you probably won't. Nothing is too far-fetched when you trust in Me and strive for greatness through Me. Read the Bible and see all the incredible things I want you to accomplish. Dream big and live large for Me.

You are more than a conqueror,

Your Heavenly Father

> Dear brothers, I am still not all I should be but I am bringing all my energies to bear on this one thing: Forgetting the past and looking forward to what lies ahead.
>
> PHILIPPIANS 3:13 TLB

God never changes his mind about the people he calls and the things he gives them.
ROMANS 11:29 NCV

To this end also we pray for you always, that our God will count you worthy of your calling, and fulfill every desire for goodness and the work of faith with power.
2 THESSALONIANS 1:11 NASB

Who hath saved us, and called *us* with an holy calling, not according to our works, but according to his own purpose and grace, which was given us in Christ Jesus before the world began.
2 TIMOTHY 1:9

You are a chosen people, royal priests, a holy nation, a people for God's own possession. You were chosen to tell about the wonderful acts of God, who called you out of darkness into his wonderful light.
1 PETER 2:9 NCV

Brothers and sisters, use more effort to make God's calling and choosing of you secure. If you keep doing this, you will never fall away.
2 PETER 1:10 GOD'S WORD

Goals

WORKING FROM A CLEAN SLATE

Just ask for My forgiveness.

My Son,

Do you know how far the east is from the west? It goes on and on and does not end. That is how far I remove your sins from you once you repent and seek My forgiveness.

I have forgiven children who have taken a cookie when they were told not to eat it, and I have forgiven individuals who have done terrible things to their fellow man. To human eyes the penitents look very different, but not to Me. Anyone who comes to Me seeking My forgiveness walks away spotless in My eyes.

Come to Me and seek My forgiveness no matter what you do. I love you so much, and I want to cleanse you from your offense and wipe your slate clean.

Waiting to forgive and embrace you,

Your Loving Father

Count yourself lucky, how happy you must be—
you get a fresh start,
your slate's wiped clean.
PSALM 32:1 THE MESSAGE

Fortunate those whose crimes are carted off, whose sins are wiped clean from the slate.

ROMANS 4:7 THE MESSAGE

Moses went back to the LORD and said, "Oh, what a great sin these people have committed! They have made themselves gods of gold. But now, please forgive their sin—but if not, then blot me out of the book you have written."

EXODUS 32:31-32 NIV

The LORD, the LORD,
a God merciful and gracious,
slow to anger, and abounding
in steadfast love and faithfulness.

EXODUS 34:6 NRSV

The LORD is slow to anger and rich in unfailing love, forgiving every kind of sin and rebellion. Even so he does not leave sin unpunished, but he punishes the children for the sins of their parents to the third and fourth generations.

NUMBERS 14:18 NLT

What a difference between man's sin
and God's forgiveness!

ROMANS 5:15 TLB

Forgiveness from God

Forgiveness from God

In him we have redemption through his blood, the forgiveness of sins, in accordance with the riches of God's grace.

EPHESIANS 1:7 NIV

I am your servant, and the people of Israel belong to you. So whenever any of us look toward this temple and pray, answer from your home in heaven and forgive our sins.

1 KINGS 8:30 CEV

Hear them from heaven and forgive and answer all who have made an honest confession; for you know each heart.

1 KINGS 8:39 TLB

If My people who are called by My name will humble themselves, and pray and seek My face, and turn from their wicked ways, then I will hear from heaven, and will forgive their sin and heal their land.

2 CHRONICLES 7:14 NKJV

You, O Lord, are good and forgiving, full of mercy toward everyone who calls out to you.

PSALM 86:5 GOD'S WORD

"Father, forgive these people," Jesus said, "for they don't know what they are doing." And the soldiers gambled for his clothing, throwing dice for each piece.

LUKE 23:34 TLB

But you forgive us, and so we will
worship you.
PSALM 130:4 CEV

Don't judge others, and God won't judge
you. Don't be hard on others, and God
won't be hard on you. Forgive others,
and God will forgive you.
LUKE 6:37 CEV

Be ye kind one to another, tenderhearted,
forgiving one another, even as God for
Christ's sake hath forgiven you.
EPHESIANS 4:32

God used his power to give Jesus the
highest position as leader and savior. He did
this to lead the people of Israel to him, to
change the way they think and act,
and to forgive their sins.
ACTS 5:31 GOD'S WORD

The Son paid for our sins,
and in him we have forgiveness.
COLOSSIANS 1:14 NCV

Working from
a Clean Slate

ALWAYS THE BEST OPTION

Honesty is like a diamond in the rough.

My Own,

In the business world, there is not a character trait more valuable than honesty. An honest man can get deals done quickly because the other party doesn't second-guess the integrity of the transaction. If productivity ever slows, a boss believes the reasons that an honest man gives, because he knows that the worker is not simply throwing excuses around. And co-workers don't worry about gossip or backstabbing from an honest man.

The book of Proverbs says that the godly are directed by their honesty. May you always see how important your honesty is, and may others follow your lead so that your life at home and at work will be more pleasurable.

Filling you with integrity,

God, Who Is Truth

Let us walk honestly, as in the day; not in rioting and drunkenness, not in chambering and wantonness, not in strife and envying.

ROMANS 13:13

You will be respected by people who are not followers of the Lord, and you won't have to depend on anyone.
1 THESSALONIANS 4:12 CEV

Pray for us; for we are confident that we have a good conscience, in all things desiring to live honorably.
HEBREWS 13:18 NKJV

The *seed* in the good soil, these are the ones who have heard the word in an honest and good heart, and hold it fast, and bear fruit with perseverance.
LUKE 8:15 NASB

Brothers and sisters, keep your thoughts on whatever is right or deserves praise: things that are true, honorable, fair, pure, acceptable, or commendable.
PHILIPPIANS 4:8 GOD'S WORD

It is because I have preached these great truths that I am in trouble here and have been put in jail like a criminal. But the Word of God is not chained, even though I am.
2 TIMOTHY 2:9 TLB

Honesty

WHAT KEEPS YOU GOING

Hope is fuel for your empty tank.

Dear Son,

What drives a man to pound the pavement to look for employment the day after he loses his job? Hope. What encourages a runner to compete in a marathon every year, even though he knows he'll never win? Hope. What motivated Jesus' followers after He died on the cross? Hope.

Hope is an invaluable resource that never has to run out. It's available whenever you want it and for however long you choose to hold on to it. It's more than dreaming or wishing; it's a confident belief that everything will go according to plan when you keep your eyes focused on Me rather than on your circumstances.

From your endless supply of hope,

Father God

Lord, where do I put my hope?
My only hope is in you.
PSALM 39:7 NLT

*Anyone who is among the
living has hope—
even a live dog is better off
than a dead lion!*
ECCLESIASTES 9:4 NIV

Celebrate and sing for Israel,
the greatest of nations.
Offer praises and shout,
"Come and rescue your people, LORD!
Save what's left of Israel."
JEREMIAH 31:7 CEV

I will give back her vineyards to her, and
transform her Valley of Troubles into a Door
of Hope. She will respond to me there,
singing with joy as in days long ago in her
youth, after I had freed her
from captivity in Egypt.
HOSEA 2:15 TLB

Hoping against hope, he believed that he
would become "the father of many nations,"
according to what was said, "So numerous
shall your descendants be."
ROMANS 4:18 NRSV

Hope

Hope

I have set the LORD always before me.
Because he is at my right hand,
I shall not be shaken.
Therefore my heart is glad
and my tongue rejoices;
my body also will rest secure.
PSALM 16:8-9 NIV

I shall delight in Your statutes;
I shall not forget Your word.
PSALM 119:16 NASB

You had my mother give birth to me.
You made me trust you
while I was just a baby.
PSALM 22:9 NCV

We were saved with this hope in mind. If we hope
for something we already see, it's not really hope.
Who hopes for what can be seen? But if we hope
for what we don't see, we eagerly wait
for it with perseverance.
ROMANS 8:24-25 GOD'S WORD

Prepare your minds for action; discipline yourselves;
set all your hope on the grace that Jesus Christ will
bring you when he is revealed.
1 PETER 1:13 NRSV

Be joyful in hope, patient in affliction,
faithful in prayer.

ROMANS 12:12 NIV

Be strong and take courage,
all you who put your hope in the LORD!

PSALM 31:24 NLT

Why am I so sad?
Why am I so upset?
I should put my hope in God
and keep praising him,
my Savior and my God.

PSALM 42:11 NCV

Why are you down in the dumps, dear soul?
Why are you crying the blues?
Fix my eyes on God—
soon I'll be praising again.
He puts a smile on my face.
He's my God.

PSALM 43:5 THE MESSAGE

Blessed are those who trust in the LORD,
whose trust is the LORD.

JEREMIAH 17:7 NRSV

What Keeps
You Going

DEFLECTING ALL PRAISE TO ME

Give credit where credit is due.

My Own,

Tell Me if you think this would be fair:

A businessman develops a plan that, when implemented, will entirely transform his company. He gets his fellow employees on board, and they hit the road running with this new strategy. Well, it works, and the company does indeed prosper. But when the time comes for accolades to be passed out, a different person steps forward and takes credit for the successful transformation.

This happens to Me all the time. I want My children to succeed, but when they do, I want others to know about My provision, My strength, and My wisdom in bringing about change. It's okay to be proud of your accomplishments—just remember to give Me the praise.

Always there for you,

Almighty God

My soul shall make her boast in the LORD: the humble shall hear *thereof*, and be glad.
PSALM 34:2

Whoever exalts himself will be humbled, and he who humbles himself will be exalted.
MATTHEW 23:12 NKJV

Respect and serve the LORD!
Your reward will be wealth,
a long life, and honor.
PROVERBS 22:4 CEV

Better poor and humble than proud and rich.
PROVERBS 16:19 TLB

Far below him are the heavens and the earth.
He stoops to look,
and he lifts the poor from the dirt
and the needy from the garbage dump.
He sets them among princes,
even the princes of his own people!
PSALM 113:6-8 NLT

What he gives in love is far better than
anything else you'll find. It's common
knowledge that "God goes against the
willful proud; God gives grace
to the willing humble."
JAMES 4:6 THE MESSAGE

Humility

FOLLOWING MY MARCHING ORDERS

You're in the Lord's army.

Dear Soldier,

In the heat of battle, a general doesn't bark out his orders just because he has the power and position to do so. Instead, he knows better than anyone else the objectives that must be identified and the strategy that must be followed to assure victory for his troops. But if one man decides to step outside of the general's plan, he compromises the whole platoon.

Since the day you decided to follow Me, you have been enlisted in My army. Always remember the words to the song that little boys have sung for more than a century— "Onward Christian soldiers, marching as to war"—and keep your eyes focused on Me, your Commanding Officer.

Together we will fight the good fight,

The Lord, Who Is a Warrior

You will be blessed if you obey the commands of the Lord your God that I am giving you today.
DEUTERONOMY 11:27 NCV

The sacrifice that honors me is a
thankful heart. Obey me,
and I, your God, will show
my power to save.
PSALM 50:23 CEV

Be on your guard before him and obey his
voice; do not be rebellious toward him, for
he will not pardon your transgression, since
My name is in him.
EXODUS 23:21 NASB

Don't you know that you are slaves of
anyone you obey? You can be slaves of sin
and die, or you can be obedient slaves of God
and be acceptable to him.
ROMANS 6:16 CEV

Then Peter and the *other* apostles answered
and said, We ought to obey God
rather than men.
ACTS 5:29

"Be sure to continue to obey all of the
commandments Moses gave you. Love the
Lord and follow his plan for your lives. Cling
to him and serve him enthusiastically."
JOSHUA 22:5 TLB

Obedience

Obedience

God the Father has his eye on each of you, and has determined by the work of the Spirit to keep you obedient through the sacrifice of Jesus. May everything good from God be yours!
1 PETER 1:2 THE MESSAGE

Remember today, and never forget that the LORD is God in heaven above and here on earth. There is no other god. Obey his laws and commands which I'm giving you today. Then things will go well for you and your descendants. You will live for a long time in the land. The LORD your God is giving you the land for as long as you live.
DEUTERONOMY 4:39-40 GOD'S WORD

Through Christ, all the kindness of God has been poured out upon us undeserving sinners; and now he is sending us out around the world to tell all people everywhere the great things God has done for them, so that they, too, will believe and obey him.
ROMANS 1:5 TLB

His inward affection is more abundant toward you, whilst he remembereth the obedience of you all, how with fear and trembling ye received him.
2 CORINTHIANS 7:15

Now to God who is able to strengthen you according to my gospel and the proclamation of Jesus Christ, according to the revelation of the mystery that was kept secret for long ages but is now disclosed, and through the prophetic writings is made known to all the Gentiles, according to the command of the eternal God, to bring about the obedience of faith.

ROMANS 16:25-26 NRSV

Let us who live in the light think clearly, protected by the body armor of faith and love, and wearing as our helmet the confidence of our salvation.

1 THESSALONIANS 5:8 NLT

Study this Book of the Law continually. Meditate on it day and night so you may be sure to obey all that is written in it. Only then will you succeed.

JOSHUA 1:8 NLT

Ye see your calling, brethren, how that not many wise men after the flesh, not many mighty, not many noble, *are called*.

1 CORINTHIANS 1:26

Following My
Marching Orders

DOING RIGHT AT ALL TIMES

Live honorably even when alone.

My Own,

I know that it's easier to live a virtuous life when others around you are doing so. You know what you should and shouldn't do as My follower, and you don't want to mislead or disappoint anyone. But I want you to be that steadfast at all times—not because I can still see everything that you do, but because you know and do the right thing.

If you develop and follow godly principles when you are in private, you will possess an integrity that remains intact at all times. Living a fervent Christian life will become as natural as breathing is to you.

Directing your steps,

Your Heavenly Father

> You yourselves are our witnesses—as is
> God—that we have been pure and honest and
> faultless toward every one of you.
> 1 THESSALONIANS 2:10 TLB

I guide you in the way of wisdom and lead you along straight paths.
PROVERBS 4:11 NIV

Do what is right and good in the LORD's sight,
so that it may go well with you and you may
go in and take over the good land that the
LORD promised on oath to your forefathers.
DEUTERONOMY 6:18 NIV

You shall remove the guilt of innocent blood
from your midst, when you do what is right in
the eyes of the LORD.
DEUTERONOMY 21:9 NASB

You shall not eat it, that it may go well with
you and your children after you, when you do
what is right in the sight of the LORD.
DEUTERONOMY 12:25 NKJV

God, make a fresh start in me,
shape a Genesis week from the chaos
of my life.
PSALM 51:10 THE MESSAGE

Integrity

KEEP ALL THINGS IN PERSPECTIVE

Never let eternity out of your sight.

Dear Son,

I know, and you know, that life is much more than a game—it is also an adventure, a battle, a life-and-death situation. It's helpful to think of life in terms that are familiar.

Think about a NASCAR race. Every driver starts out at the green flag and fully intends to capture the checkered one at the finish line. He may have a terrible starting position, yet he remains undaunted. He may have problems with a tire, yet he maintains his pursuit. He may get bumped from behind and the side, but he still keeps focused on his goal: the checkered flag.

You, too, face challenges in life. Some may seem insurmountable. But never lose sight of the finish line: eternal life with Me.

You can win the race! Don't give up!

The God Who Saves

Eternal life is to know you, the only true God,
and to know Jesus Christ, the one you sent.
JOHN 17:3 CEV

Jesus answered and said unto him,
Verily, verily, I say unto thee,
Except a man be born again, he
cannot see the kingdom of God.
JOHN 3:3

Let what you heard from the beginning abide
in you. If what you heard from the beginning
abides in you, then you will abide in the Son
and in the Father. And this is what he has
promised us, eternal life.

1 JOHN 2:24-25 NRSV

Keep yourselves in God's love as you wait for
the mercy of our Lord Jesus Christ to bring
you to eternal life.

JUDE 21 NIV

A new heart also will I give you, and a new
spirit will I put within you: and I will take
away the stony heart out of your flesh, and I
will give you an heart of flesh.

EZEKIEL 36:26

You have been born again, and this new life
did not come from something that dies, but
from something that cannot die. You were
born again through God's living message that
continues forever.

1 PETER 1:23 NCV

Salvation

Salvation

Those who eat my flesh and drink my blood have eternal life, and I will raise them at the last day.
JOHN 6:54 NLT

We have seen with our own eyes and now tell all the world that God sent his Son to be their Savior. Anyone who believes and says that Jesus is the Son of God has God living in him, and he is living with God.
1 JOHN 4:14-15 TLB

Whoever believes that Jesus is the Christ is born of God, and everyone who loves Him who begot also loves him who is begotten of Him.
1 JOHN 5:1 NKJV

Make no mistake: In the end you get what's coming to you—*Real Life* for those who work on God's side.
ROMANS 2:7 THE MESSAGE

The payment for sin is death, but the gift that God freely gives is everlasting life found in Christ Jesus our Lord.
ROMANS 6:23 GOD'S WORD

I give them eternal life, and they will never perish. No one will snatch them out of my hand.
JOHN 10:28 NRSV

We know that anyone born of God does not continue to sin; the one who was born of God keeps him safe, and the evil one cannot harm him.

1 JOHN 5:18 NIV

God says,
"At the right time I heard your prayers.
On the day of salvation I helped you."
I tell you that the "right time" is now, and the "day of salvation" is now.

2 CORINTHIANS 6:2 NCV

Therefore, since we are surrounded by so great a cloud of witnesses, let us also lay aside every weight and the sin that clings so closely, and let us run with perseverance the race that is set before us.

HEBREWS 12:1 NRSV

I pray also that the eyes of your heart may be enlightened in order that you may know the hope to which he has called you, the riches of his glorious inheritance in the saints.

EPHESIANS 1:18 NIV

Keep All Things in Perspective

ENJOY MY CREATION

I made this beautiful earth for you.

My Creation,

Please give heed to the old saying "Stop and smell the roses." While it is just a figure of speech, why not take it literally? While you're at it, walk barefoot through the grass, climb a tall tree, stomp through a rain puddle, and chase a grasshopper. Enjoy My creation more.

When I was creating the earth, I could hardly wait to finish and make you, because I knew how much you would love all that you would see and touch and smell and taste. Take time today to enjoy your beautiful surroundings. See the world as a little child does, and look for something to explore.

May you always enjoy your world,

The Creator of Heaven and Earth

God saw every thing that he had made, and, behold, *it was* very good. And the evening and the morning were the sixth day.
GENESIS 1:31

The God of gods, the LORD, speaks.
He calls the earth from the
rising to the setting sun.
God shines from Jerusalem,
whose beauty is perfect.
PSALM 50:1-2 NCV

Tell those who are rich in this world not to
be proud and not to trust in their money,
which will soon be gone. But their trust
should be in the living God, who richly gives
us all we need for our enjoyment.
1 TIMOTHY 6:17 NLT

No one will take away their
homes or vineyards.
My chosen people will live to be as
old as trees, and they will enjoy
what they have earned.
ISAIAH 65:22 CEV

The LORD God made all kinds of trees grow
out of the ground—trees that were pleasing
to the eye and good for food.
GENESIS 2:9 NIV

The heavens tell of the glory of God.
The skies display his marvelous craftmanship.
PSALM 19:1 NLT

Nature

PASSING ALONG GRACE

Forgive others as I forgive you.

My Joy,

I love to give you gifts. The gift that I most like to give is My grace to you. When you least expect it—and when you know for sure that you are not worthy—I love to forgive and bless you. You should see the look on your face when you receive My grace. Your reaction is a joy for me.

I want you to do likewise to those around you. In fact, that is one thing I require of you—to forgive others as I have forgiven you. The next time someone does something mean to you, don't respond in kind. Rather, go out of your way to astound him with something he doesn't deserve: grace.

With grace that is greater than all your sins,

Your Heavenly Father

"Love your enemies! Pray for those who persecute you!"
MATTHEW 5:44 NLT

*Keep us forgiven with you and
forgiving others.
Keep us safe from ourselves
and the Devil.*

LUKE 11:4 THE MESSAGE

"Thus you shall say to Joseph, 'Please forgive,
I beg you, the transgression of your brothers
and their sin, for they did you wrong.' And
now, please forgive the transgression of the
servants of the God of your father." And
Joseph wept when they spoke to him.

GENESIS 50:17 NASB

If you are offering your gift at the altar and
remember there that another believer has
something against you, leave your gift at the
altar. First go away and make peace with that
person. Then come back and offer your gift.

MATTHEW 5:23-24 GOD'S WORD

Love your enemies, do good to them, and
lend to them without hoping to get anything
back. Then you will have a great reward, and
you will be children of the Most High God,
because he is kind even to people who are
ungrateful and full of sin.

LUKE 6:35 NCV

Forgiveness of Others

Forgiveness of Others

*Whenever you stand praying, forgive, if you have
anything against anyone; so that your Father in
heaven may also forgive you your trespasses.*
MARK 11:25 NRSV

Even if one of them mistreats you seven times in
one day and says, "I am sorry," you should still
forgive that person.
LUKE 17:4 CEV

Now it is time to forgive him and comfort him.
Otherwise he may become so bitter and
discouraged that he won't be able to recover.
2 CORINTHIANS 2:7 TLB

Speak and act as those who are going to be judged
by the law that gives freedom, because judgment
without mercy will be shown to anyone who has
not been merciful. Mercy triumphs over judgment!
JAMES 2:12-13 NIV

Bearing with one another, and forgiving one
another, if anyone has a complaint against another;
even as Christ forgave you, so you also *must do.*
COLOSSIANS 3:13 NKJV

Bless those who persecute you;
bless and do not curse.
ROMANS 12:14 NASB

"Forgive us for our sins,
just as we have forgiven
those who sinned against us.
And do not cause us to be tempted,
but save us from the Evil One."
Yes, if you forgive others for their sins, your
Father in heaven will also forgive you for
your sins.

MATTHEW 6:12-14 NCV

Likewise shall my heavenly Father do also
unto you, if ye from your hearts forgive not
every one his brother their trespasses.

MATTHEW 18:35

If ye forgive not men their trespasses,
neither will your Father forgive your
trespasses.

MATTHEW 6:15

My friends, do not try to punish others
when they wrong you, but wait for God to
punish them with his anger. It is written: "I
will punish those who do wrong; I will repay
them," says the Lord.

ROMANS 12:19 NCV

Passing Along
Grace

NEVER GIVE UP

Accomplish what you set out to do.

Dear Son,

What if Abraham Lincoln had given up running for political office after many early defeats? What if Dr. Seuss had given up writing for children after dozens of book rejections? What if the apostle Peter had given up his faith after his three-time denial of Jesus? One, they would not have reaped great success from their persistent sowing of many seeds. Two, they would not have touched so dramatically the lives of millions of people.

The next time you are faced with a setback, don't entertain the idea of relinquishing your dreams and your calling in life. Though you may fail today, success is around the corner for those who persevere.

With My strength to lead you on,

Almighty God

> Without wavering, let us hold tightly to the hope we say we have, for God can be trusted to keep his promise.
> HEBREWS 10:23 NLT

Finish what you started in me, God.
Your love is eternal—don't quit
on me now.
PSALM 138:8 THE MESSAGE

Moses indeed was faithful in all His house as a
servant, for a testimony of those things which
would be spoken *afterward*, but Christ as a
Son over His own house, whose house we
are if we hold fast the confidence and the
rejoicing of the hope firm to the end.
HEBREWS 3:5-6 NKJV

You must encourage one another each day.
And you must keep on while there is still a
time that can be called "today." If you don't,
then sin may fool some of you
and make you stubborn.
HEBREWS 3:13 CEV

Nevertheless what you have,
hold fast until I come.
REVELATION 2:25 NASB

The person who is right with me
will live by trusting in me.
But if he turns back with fear,
I will not be pleased with him.
HEBREWS 10:38 NCV

Perseverance

A HEART READY TO BURST

You have been blessed.

Dearest One,

A little girl got her first ride on a John Deere mower one day—an opportunity for her to "help" cut the grass. She had been looking forward to it for weeks, and the day had finally come. As she and her daddy motored around the yard, she squealed with glee and blurted out, "This is the best life ever!" How true are those words. This is the best life ever, because it is the life I have given you.

Without even realizing it, many adults cruise through life missing countless opportunities to be grateful for all that they have. If you slow down enough to recognize the many blessings I have given to you, you, too, will blurt out your praise and thanks to Me.

With a well of blessing that will never run dry,

Your Heavenly Father

Thank the God of all gods,
His love never quits.
PSALM 136:2 THE MESSAGE

*Let us praise the Lord
together, and exalt his name.*
PSALM 34:3 TLB

Offer unto God thanksgiving; and pay thy
vows unto the most High: And call upon me
in the day of trouble: I will deliver thee, and
thou shalt glorify me.

PSALM 50:14-15

He commanded the multitude to sit down on
the ground. And He took the seven loaves
and gave thanks, broke *them* and gave *them*
to His disciples to set before *them;* and they
set *them* before the multitude.

MARK 8:6 NKJV

Jesus took the loaves, gave thanks to God,
and passed them out to the people.
Afterward he did the same with the fish. And
they all ate until they were full.

JOHN 6:11 NLT

He broke the bread, gave thanks to God,
passed it around, and they all ate heartily.

ACTS 27:35 THE MESSAGE

Thankfulness

Thankfulness

These living creatures give glory, honor, and thanks to the One who sits on the throne, who lives forever and ever.
REVELATION 4:9 NCV

All the angels were standing around the throne and around the elders and the four living beings. And they fell face down before the throne and worshiped God. They said,
"Amen! Blessing and glory and wisdom and thanksgiving and honor and power and strength belong to our God forever and forever. Amen!"
REVELATION 7:11-12 NLT

Thanks be to God, who gives us the victory through our Lord Jesus Christ.
1 CORINTHIANS 15:57 NRSV

At that very moment she came up and *began* giving thanks to God, and continued to speak of Him to all those who were looking for the redemption of Jerusalem.
LUKE 2:38 NASB

Let them sacrifice thank offerings and tell of his works with songs of joy.
PSALM 107:22 NIV

Sing to the LORD! Praise his name!
Day after day announce that the
LORD saves his people.
Tell people about his glory.
Tell all the nations about his miracles.
PSALM 96:2-3 GOD'S WORD

Everything God created is good. And if you
give thanks, you may eat anything.
1 TIMOTHY 4:4 CEV

This service you do not only helps the needs
of God's people, it also brings many more
thanks to God.
2 CORINTHIANS 9:12 NCV

Continue in prayer, and watch in the
same with thanksgiving.
COLOSSIANS 4:2

He who regards one day as special, does so
to the Lord. He who eats meat, eats to the
Lord, for he gives thanks to God; and he
who abstains, does so to the Lord and gives
thanks to God.
ROMANS 14:6 NIV

A Heart Ready
to Burst

Seek This at Any Cost

Don't waste time chasing imposters.

Dear Son,

The truth shall set you free. You've heard that phrase before. The opposite is also true: if you do not have the truth in you, then you are in bondage, unable to live the life you were meant to live. Where do you find that truth? In Me. I am the Way, the Truth, and the Life.

So you see, truth is much more than simply getting the facts straight or not telling a lie. It is all about knowing—knowing that I am God, knowing that I have a plan for you, and knowing that there is no other place you'd rather be than abiding in Me.

With Me you're free indeed,

Eternal God

I have chosen the way of truth;
I have set my heart on your laws.
PSALM 119:30 NIV

*Walk straight,
act right, tell the truth.*
PSALM 15:2
THE MESSAGE

He shall cover thee with his feathers, and
under his wings shalt thou trust: his truth
shall be thy shield and buckler.
PSALM 91:4

PRAISE THE LORD, all nations everywhere.
Praise him, all the peoples of the earth. For
he loves us very dearly, and his truth endures.
Praise the Lord.
PSALM 117 TLB

Tell the truth to each other. Render
verdicts in your courts that are just and that
lead to peace.
ZECHARIAH 8:16 NLT

The Word became a human and lived among
us. We saw his glory—the glory that belongs
to the only Son of the Father—and he was
full of grace and truth.
JOHN 1:14 NCV

Truth

The Faithful Promises of God

*Let the peace of God rule in your hearts, to which
also you were called in one body; and be thankful.*
COLOSSIANS 3:15 NKJV

These things I have written to you who believe in
the name of the Son of God, so that you may know
that you have eternal life.
1 JOHN 5:13 NASB

I will instruct you and teach you in the way you
should go; I will counsel you and watch over you.
PSALM 32:8 NIV

Those who know your name trust in you, for you,
O LORD, have never abandoned anyone who
searches for you.
PSALM 9:10 NLT

Be anxious for nothing, but in everything by prayer
and supplication with thanksgiving let your requests
be made know to God.
PHILIPPIANS 4:6 NASB

Wait on the LORD: be of good courage, and he shall
strengthen thine heart: wait, I say, on the LORD.
PSALM 27:14

When I am afraid, I put my trust in you.

PSALM 56:3 NLT

We do not lose heart. Though outwardly
we are wasting away, yet inwardly we are
being renewed day by day. For our light and
momentary troubles are achieving for us an
eternal glory that far outweighs them all. So
we fix our eyes not on what is seen, but on
what is unseen. For what is seen is
temporary, but what is unseen is eternal.

2 CORINTHIANS 4:16-18 NIV

I will walk before the LORD
In the land of the living.

PSALM 116:9 NASB

God will surely do this for you, for he
always does just what he says, and he is the
one who invited you in to this wonderful
friendship with his Son, even Christ
our LORD.

1 CORINTHIANS 1:9 TLB

Thank You, God

If you have enjoyed this book, we invite
you to visit our website to learn about
other Harvest House books and products:

www.harvesthousepublishers.com

HARVEST HOUSE PUBLISHERS

EUGENE, OREGON